language in colour

Themes for infants and lower juniors with poetry as the starting-point

Moira Andrew

Newlyn Bay

We look down on
fishing boats
t
e
t
h
e
r
e
d
to the harbour wall,
their riding lights
flickering
like fireflies
in the summer dark.

They dip and curtsey
like a corps de ballet

d a n c i n g

to the tune
of the waves.

Moira Andrew

Illustrations by Kathie Barrs

First published in 1989
Reprinted 1990
BELAIR PUBLICATIONS LIMITED
P.O. Box 12. Twickenham, England, TW1 2QL

Series Editor Robyn Gordon
Designed by Richard Souper
Photography by David Hume & Associates
Cover photography by Kelvin Freeman
Typesetting by Tameside Filmsetting Ltd,
Printed and Bound by Heanor Gate Printing Limited
ISBN 0 947882 10 3

Acknowledgements

The author and publishers would like to thank the Headteacher, children and staff of the Severn Beach County Primary school, Severn Beach, for their co-operation and generous contributions towards the display work in this book.

They would also like to thank Trafalgar School, Twickenham, for permission to include the wild flower display on page 9.

The author would also like to thank the Craigie College of Education, Ayr, where she was first introduced to the idea of using poetry as a curriculum resource.

The author and publishers wish to thank the following who have kindly given permission for the use of copyright material.

Dave Calder for 'Flowers are soft' and 'Flood'

Carcanet Press Ltd. for 'This is Just to Say' by William Carlos Williams from *Collected Poems 1909-1939*, eds. Litz and MacGowan

Tony Charles for 'Snails'

Collins Publishers for 'The Frozen Man' from *Rabbiting On* by Kit Wright

John Cotton for 'Wave', 'Frost' and 'Fog' from *The Crystal Zoo*, OUP; and 'Greengrocer', 'Dragonfly', 'Exploring the rock pool' and 'Snow'

Sue Cowling for 'The Creek'

Edna Eglinton for 'Breakfast in the Harbour'

Faber and Faber Ltd. for 'Winter' from *Midnight Forest* by Judith Nicholls

John Fairfax for 'Pictures from a Harbour' and 'Water All Around'

John Foster for 'The Sea', 'The River', 'My Shadow', 'The Storm', 'When the wind blows', 'Overnight', 'What is fog?' and 'This morning my dad shouted', Copyright 1989 by John Foster

Michael Henry for 'Lammas Loaf' and 'Christmas Album'

Geoffrey Holloway for an extract from 'Sweet Peas' in *The Crones of Aphrodite*, Free Man's Press Editions Ltd., 1985; 'daddy long legs', 'Sun', 'wind's a funny old thing', 'Millionaire' and 'There's an old window cleaner'

Jean Kenward for 'Sunflowers', 'The Garden', 'Winter Gulls', 'The Harbour', 'Rain' and 'Old Winter'

Ian McMillan for 'The fog and me'

Wes Magee for 'The harbour wall', 'The pond', 'The waterfall', 'When I went fishing', 'Summer sun' and 'Three taps'

Gerda Mayer for 'Grumpy and Gruff'

Judith Nicholls for 'What's the time, Mr Dandelion?' from *Popcorn Pie*, Mary Glasgow Publications. Copyright 1988 Judith Nicholls; and 'Water's for . . .'. Copyright 1988 Judith Nicholls

Penguin Books Ltd. for 'The hardest thing in the world to do' by Michael Rosen from *You Tell Me*, eds. Roger McGough and Michael Rosen, Viking Kestrel Books, Copyright 1979 Michael Rosen; and 'Poem of Solitary Delight' by Tachibana Akemi from *The Penguin Book of Japanese Verse*, trans. Geoffrey Bownes and Anthony Thwaite, Penguin Books 1964, Copyright 1964 Geoffrey Bownes and Anthony Thwaite.

Patricia Pogson for 'Cornflowers', 'Primary' and 'haiku'

Joan Poulson for 'golden-growing on the hill' and 'a puddle-skrinkling day'

Irene Rawnsley for 'Cress on a Saucer', 'Seed Songs', 'On a windy day' and 'On the lawn one morning'

Marian Reiner on behalf of the author for 'Yellow Weed' from *Little Racoon and Poems from the Woods* by Lilian Moore. Copyright 1975 by Lilian Moore

Penelope Rieu for 'The Paint Box' by E. V. Rieu

Maurice Rutherford for 'Strikebound' from *The Unicorn and Lion*, Macmillan Education, 1987. Copyright 1987 Maurice Rutherford

Sheila Simmons for 'Snowy Day in the Park' from *Another First Poetry Book*, ed. John Foster, Oxford University Press

Sue Stewart for 'River Recipe'

John Walsh for 'Insects'

Dave Ward for 'Sunshine', 'When the Wind Blows', 'It's only the storm' and 'Fog'

The publishers also wish to thank Moira Andrew for 'shower' from *The First Lick of the Lolly*, Macmillan Education; 'Raspberry Jam' from *A Shooting Star*, ed. Wes Magee, Basil Blackwell; 'Any Colour as long as it's white', *Living Language*, BBC; 'Mid-Summer Feast' from *My Red Poetry Book*, Macmillan Education

Every effort has been made to trace all the copyright holders but if any have been inadvertently overlooked the publishers will be pleased to make the necessary arrangement at the first opportunity.

Contents

Introduction

All good primary schools make the development of language a fundamental aim. Now that language has been defined as one of the three main subject areas in the National Curriculum, it has a very high profile indeed. *Language in Colour* is a collection of teaching ideas designed to encourage children to practise and develop their skills in listening and speaking, reading and writing.

The themes in this book relate closely to the children's own environment, and each is introduced by a page of poems to enrich and deepen the child's experience and understanding of the topic. Poetry is a valuable curriculum resource, and *Language in Colour* aims to use the rich language of poetry as a starting-point from which teachers can create a learning experience across the curriculum for children in the early years of the primary school.

It is hoped that the ideas in this book will help teachers in their task of creating a stimulating environment where children can express themselves as fully as possible in speaking and writing. The children can work either from their own direct experience, or from an interest in the poem outward into the environment. There is no *correct* method, and the suggestions are open-ended. Teachers can dip into the book; using, discarding and developing the ideas at will. It is to be hoped that they will encourage children to explore anthologies in the classroom and library to find many more poems on the various themes.

Effective listening is an important skill. This book aims to encourage children to listen creatively, so that it becomes an active process. They listen to the poems, and build pictures in their minds, at the same time extending the range of their own skills. Both in the classroom and on outside visits the children are encouraged to listen to the sounds of the everyday environment, from the rhythms of the rain to the song in the sea-shell.

It is important to recognise the role of children's fiction and poetry in fostering language and learning. An underlying principle of this book is just this link between literature and learning, and poetry is used as a basis for talking, reading and writing. The children's skills in language are deepened and extended through interest and pleasure.

Language in Colour offers many opportunities for children to behave like real writers; to write in a variety of styles and for different purposes. Using their own experience of a topic, and having developed this through reading, talking and listening, children are asked to write poems, letters, reports and stories. The book also has a cross-curricula bias, suggesting links with art, drama and movement.

Moira Andrew
1989

GARDENS

Flowers

Yellow weed

How did you get here,
weed?
Who brought your seed?

Did it lift
on the wind and
sail
and drift
from a far and yellow
field?

Was your seed a
burr,
a sticky burr that
clung to a
fox's
furry tail?

Did it fly with a
bird
who liked to feed
on the tasty
seed
of the yellow
weed?
How did you come?

Lilian Moore

Sweet peas

They take the air
like the tossed silk
handkerchiefs
a conjuror finds
in our amazed pockets.

Part of a poem by
Geoffrey Holloway

Poem of solitary delight

What a delight it is
When of a morning,
I get up and go out
To find in full bloom a flower
That yesterday was not there.

Tachibana Akemi

Flowers are soft, they smell of aunties;
weeds are better – no-one shouts
if you pull off all their petals
or stamp them flat into the ground.

Grown-ups are funny about the garden,
they don't see it like I do –
'Such lovely flowers', they say, but really
it's a jungle where toy soldiers hide.

Leaves are alright, you can kick them,
and make smoke signals when they burn,
but what I like best in a garden
is trees to climb, fat slugs, and worms.

Dave Calder

Sunflowers

Plant a sunflower
in a pot . . .
How many sunflowers
have you got?
Wet each one
a little bit –
pour some water
over it –
When the seeds
are deep inside,
yellow petals
spreading wide
soon will grow
as tall as you!
Hello, sunflower,
How do you do?

Jean Kenward

Flowers

Discussion and Observation:

- Talk about flowers through the seasons. Identify as many as possible from catalogues, photographs, seed packets, garden and wild flower books and, if possible, the real thing.
- Look at shape and colour of petals and leaves. Feel the texture of leaves and stem.
- Smell the flowers to find out which ones have a perfume.
- Talk about how different flowers grow – from seeds, bulbs, perennials, annuals.
- Talk about roots, and how plants need sun and rain to make them grow.
- Try to imagine a world without flowers – parched, dry and lacking in colour. Talk about what happens to many of our plants in winter time. Where do our flowers come from during the winter?

Visits:

- It may be possible to visit a nearby park or a garden centre. Look inside the greenhouse and see how plants are made ready for planting out.
- Go on an organised walk to look at gardens in the roads close to school. See what flowers are in bloom at different seasons of the year. Ask a local gardener to come into school and talk about his plants and flowers.
- In the summer many areas organise a flower show. It might be possible to take the children along to such an event.
- The children may be able to visit the local church to see the flowers being arranged for a service.

Classroom Activities:

1. On a sunny day, get the children to bring in bunches of daisies. Make lots of daisy chains. Let them hang them round their necks and wrists.
2. Bring flowers into school. Sort them into garden flowers/wild flowers/weeds. Make a flower calendar.
3. Look closely at the colour of one flower. Is the colour of each petal the same? Does the colour vary as the flower grows from bud to full bloom and fades? (See Patricia Pogson's poem 'Cornflower' in the Colour section.) Look at the shapes of whole flowers, of separate petals, of leaves.
4. Look at the pattern/patches of colour made by massed flowers growing in the park and on traffic roundabouts, or bunched ready for sale in the flower shops. (See Creative Activities.)
5. Listen to the rustling of flowers and leaves in the wind, to seeds rattling, e.g. poppy seeds. Listen to bees buzzing among the flowers.
6. Look at the movement of flowers in a gentle breeze/in a strong wind. Think how destructive a storm can be.
7. The children might make pot-pourri.
8. The children can be encouraged to sow and raise wild flower seeds. They might plant the seedlings out in a wild garden. They will enjoy working in the garden and parents might be recruited to help.
9. Keep a wild flower/wild garden diary.

Flowers

10. Press flowers, leaves and grasses between sheets of blotting paper or newspaper, weighted by heavy books.

    After several days the pressed flowers can be mounted in nature diaries, or arranged to make cards and flower pictures.

Language Activities:

1. Read Lilian Moore's 'Yellow weed'. Imagine that you have found a magic seed. Plant it and tell what happens. Will it grow into a great beanstalk like Jack's? Will it grow lots of different-shaped flowers on one stalk? Will they be in different colours? Imagine that your magic seed grows into a huge tree that has birthday cakes, jellies, ice-creams, packets of crisps and hamburgers instead of flowers.
2. When you scuff your new shoes or tear your best jumper, has your mother ever said to you 'Do you think clothes grow on trees?' Imagine a weird garden where clothes do grow on trees and bushes. Imagine choosing socks from the sock tree, pyjamas from the pyjama plant. Would your garden become a market stall or a big department store? What would the neighbours say? Make a newspaper advertisement for your new-style 'clothes' garden centre.
3. Choose your own favourite flower. Look closely at it: shape, leaves, colour. Count the petals (if there are not too many). Touch the leaves, petals, stem. Smell the flower. Turn it upside down and see how it looks now. Watch how the flower moves in the breeze. Look at Geoffrey Holloway's poem 'Sweet peas'. He says that sweet peas look like silk handkerchiefs pulled from a conjuror's pocket – and immediately you get a picture of them in your mind's eye. Find an image for your favourite flower and see if you can build a five line poem round it.

Flowers

4. Open the back door/garden gate/bedroom window to see the first hot day of summer. What do you see/smell/hear? You might be the very first person to see a flower opening its petals to the sun. (See 'Poem of solitary delight'.) Write a story or a poem called 'Open the Door' or 'Open the Gate'.
5. Read Dave Calder's poem. He doesn't think much of gardening – in fact, he says that 'Flowers are soft . . . weeds are better . . .' Make a list of the things that grown-ups like about gardens, then a list of the things *you* like about gardens. See if they match. Make up a list poem beginning 'Grown-ups are funny about the garden. . .'

Creative Activities:

1. Gather a bunch of daisies. Look at them very carefully. Use a magnifying glass so that you really get to know what a daisy looks like close up. Paint a whole page of daisies and cut them out. (See display on page 7.) Make an overlapping pattern, using as many daisies as you can, and paste them down on a background of painted grass. You could use cut and pasted tissue paper to get a different effect.
2. Read 'A poem of solitary delight'. Now use a fine brush or a pencil to make a picture of one flower which you particularly like. Keep the picture fairly small, place it in the middle of the page, with plenty of white paper round it, and make it as accurate as you can. Now, on a separate piece of paper, make a cut-out door/gate/window which opens, and paste it to the outside of your 'solitary' flower. (See Language Activities, No. 4.)

3. Make a group picture of a magic garden. Paint and cut out flower shapes. On a backdrop of trees, paste your cut-out flowers. Mix painted flowers with tissue paper/gummed paper/magazine paper shapes. Make the picture into a jungle of flowers and trees, then invent fantastic birds and insects to hide among the flowers and grasses.
4. Using a similar technique, make a group panel with magic food trees or a 'clothes' garden centre. Use felt-tip pen for the fantastic flowers/food/clothes. Cut out the shapes and glue them to the branches of the trees. Make this panel as wild and unusual as you can. Let the food/clothes shapes overlap and make it a riot of impossible colour and pattern.
5. You could make a flower pattern using potato prints. Look closely at the petal/leaf shapes and press lightly with cut potatoes dipped in paint. Overlap the petals to give the impression of full-blown flowers. Contrast the upright stems with the bunched flower heads. It might be best to choose to concentrate on a whole border of just one or two kinds of flower.
6. Visit a garden centre or a flower show. Look at the patches of colour that the massed flowers make. (See Visits). Paint the flower show, a summer flower bed or a street trader's stall with flowers massed in buckets and baskets. Go for great areas of colour, and don't try to paint individual flowers. You might think of making a collage using scraps of coloured materials and wools to give the effect of a scene bright with patches of colour.

Flowers

7. Read 'Sunflowers' by Jean Kenward. Plant nasturtiums/bean/sunflower/cress seeds. Note what happens day by day. Make a 'comic strip' to chart the progress of your plant, from seed through to flower. If you cut the pictures up into little separate pages and make them into a 'flick' book, you will see your plant 'grow' as you run your finger along the edge of the pages.
8. Use a finger-painting technique to create a summer herbaceous border. Look for round-shaped flowers like poppies, spiky ones like lupins, and for bell-shaped ones like foxgloves. Mix the shapes and heights of your flowers. Build up the shapes by dipping your finger into thick paint. Have two or three shades of one colour on a plate. It gives a lovely effect if colours run into one another on the page, so try for a range of pinks in the foxgloves, of reds in the poppies, and of greens in the leaves.

Movement and Drama:

1. Read 'Sunflowers' by Jean Kenward. Choose one child to be the gardener. The rest are seeds, lying curled and quiet deep in the soil. The 'seeds' should remember to curl with every part of their bodies, fingers, toes, spine. When the gardener 'pours some water over' the seeds, they should stretch slowly, fingers, hands, arms, until they are at full stretch, up on tiptoe. Let them nod to one another: 'Hello, sunflower/How do you do?'
2. Look at the movement of flowers in a gentle breeze/a strong wind/a storm. Think of being anchored by the roots. Sway to a gentle breeze, then a strong wind, until finally a storm comes along to uproot the flowers. Try to resist the storm, making wide slow movements with the whole body, remembering that you are rooted to the earth. Use percussion instruments to make music for the breeze/wind/storm.

Fruit & Vegetables

Raspberry jam

Take 4 lbs. of fruit.
Use whole clean berries.
Gran's script, the colour
of tea, loops its advice
across a blue-lined pad.

On summer afternoons
we ease ripe berries
from their canes,
heaping them fragrant
into a great glass bowl.

Put in pan. Add 4 lbs.
preserving sugar. Bring
slowly to the boil.
We follow instructions,
stirring in turn.

Keep to a full rolling
boil for five minutes
only. Pot up. The
heaving mass is pocked
with seed, darkens.

Just five minutes. No
more. We let it cool,
pot up into heated jars.
4 + 4 fills 9 pots! Gran's
jam defies the rules.

Moira Andrew

This is just to say

I have eaten
the plums
that were in
the icebox

and which
you were probably
saving
for breakfast

Forgive me
they were delicious
so sweet
and so cold

William Carlos Williams

Cress on a Saucer

Sleepily
seeds are unfolding
on their cottonwool bed
at the window.

Yawning,
stretching thin, silk stems
they spread little leaves
to catch the sunlight.

They smell of
warm sandwiches
eaten at holiday picnics,
in summertime.

Their taste
leaves a tingle on your tongue.

Irene Rawnsley

Greengrocer

I am a cheery greengrocer
My shop is a delight,
The apples glow and in a row
The oranges shine bright.

The onions gleam quite goldly,
While potatoes pile on pile
Reach for the sky and tell us why
The grapefruit give a smile.

Yes it is very jaunty
With its yellows, greens and brown,
So we know why the passers by
Say: 'The nicest shop in town!'

John Cotton

Fruit & Vegetables

Discussion and Observation:

- Discuss names of common fruits and vegetables, the children's likes and dislikes among these; fresh fruit, jam (What has happened to the fruit?); salads and soups; fruit juice and fruit-flavoured sweets; the way fruit and vegetables grow, and how they are cultivated.

Visits:

- Visit the local supermarket or greengrocer's shop.
- Visit the school kitchen and watch vegetables and salads being prepared.
- Visit the local church at Harvest Thanksgiving.
- Look at supermarket displays, noticing colour and shape (see Creative Activities); name and identify fruits imported into this country from abroad.
- Look at the way fruits and vegetables are displayed in the church or in school at Harvest Thanksgiving.

Fruit

Classroom Activities:

1. Look at the colour (inside and out) of apples, oranges, lemons, bananas etc.
2. Look at the difference in shape and size (e.g. grape, lemon, melon, banana).
3. Feel the shape. Feel the texture of the skin.
4. Smell oranges, lemons, apples.
5. Listen to the sound of children eating crunchy apples, juicy oranges.
6. Taste pieces of orange, lemon, grapefruit. Find words to describe taste and texture. While blind-folded, taste pieces of apple, potato, pear. Guess which is which.

Fruit & Vegetables

7. At Hallowe'en children can duck for apples.
8. Find where seeds are in each fruit. Feel them. Look at size, shape and colour.
9. Make a seed picture.
10. Plant apple seeds, orange, grapefruit and lemon pips. Try an avocado stone. Record their growth.
11. Make a graph of favourite fruits.
12. Make jam (under strict supervision). See 'Raspberry Jam'. Eat bread and home-made jam.

Vegetables

1. Look at the colour, shape and size of different vegetables, e.g. beetroot, french beans, carrots, cabbage. Cut open swede, potato, beetroot, onion, cabbage etc. and look inside. Look at the pattern inside onions, red cabbage, tomatoes etc.
2. Look at the different greens in lettuce, cabbage, leek, cauliflower, broccoli, etc. Make a chart of greens, each square getting darker every time. Find words to describe the different greens. Make a list poem of these words. (See photo on next page.)
3. Find out which vegetables grow above/on/below the soil. Make a chart of these.

4. Look at the way the outside leaves fold over and protect the inner part of the vegetable (lettuce, cauliflower, cabbage). Try to cover a tennis ball with tissue paper 'leaves'. See how neatly and carefully this must be done.
5. Smell leeks and onions. (What happens to your eyes? Find out why.)
6. Feel texture and shape of different vegetables.
7. Taste shredded lettuce and cabbage. Taste shredded carrot and swede.
8. Plant parsley/lettuce/carrot seed in the school garden or in a seedbox.
9. Plant peas and beans in glass jars with wet blotting paper. Record growth.
10. Put an onion in a bulb jar. Watch growth of roots and shoots.
11. Grow carrot tops.
12. Plant mustard and cress on blotting paper or cotton wool. Record growth. Prepare and eat mustard and cress sandwiches. (Read 'Cress on a Saucer'.)
    Plant mustard and cress in a clay 'head'. Watch the green 'hair' grow.
13. Make soup (under strict supervision). Prepare and illustrate recipes for different kinds of soup. Write a 'found' poem, using the words found in a recipe book, along with some of your own. (See 'Raspberry Jam'.)
14. Peel and boil potatoes. Eat mashed potatoes and butter. Make potato cakes.

Fruit & Vegetables

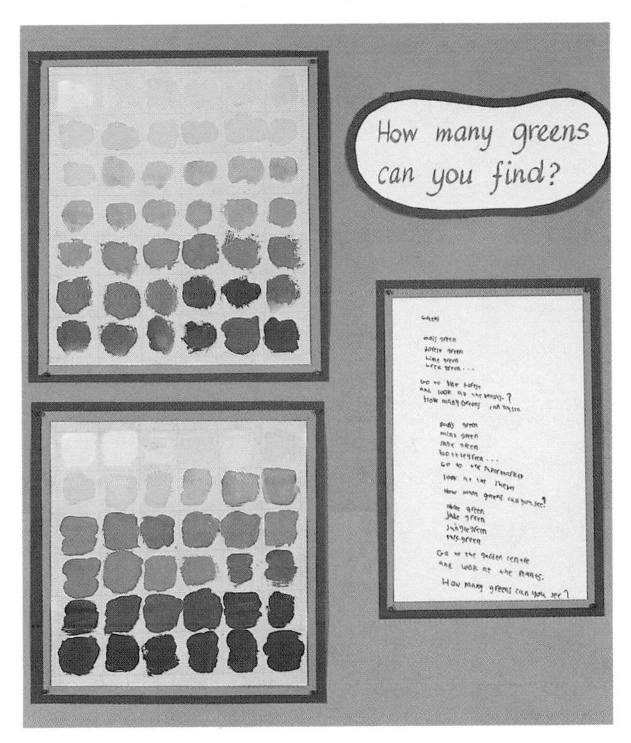

Language Activities:

1. Watch father, mother, the gardener or the caretaker working in the garden or in the park. Look at the tools needed. Make a dictionary of gardening words, e.g. digging, hoeing, raking, and of garden tools. Illustrate and/or write a description of each word, one to a page.
2. Imagine that you are a gardener. You can grow magic fruit on your trees; you can grow vegetables and flowers that nobody has ever seen before. Describe the taste, shape and smell of your new vegetables. (Do they grow on trees?) Make up names for them, then put together a catalogue to encourage other gardeners to grow them. You can be as boastful as you like about your 'new varieties'! Think of magic fruit and flowers, different from anything that has been seen before. Make and illustrate a 'Book of Magic Gardening' for the class.
3. Tell about a visit to the supermarket. Imagine that you are on your own with a shopping bag, a list and money. Tell about the smells, colours and movement in the supermarket. Listen to what people say. You might make a conversation poem between the check-out girl and yourself; an argument between a shopper and the manager; between mother and a tired child.
4. Read 'This is just to say'. Look at the way the poet has placed his words down the page. He has only used 28 words in the poem. Think of a different fruit. (You might like to put all the fruits you can think of on separate cards, and pick a card to write about.) Make your first line 'I have eaten . . .' and go on to think of finding and eating some absolutely delicious fruit which you could not resist. Think what they were being kept aside for, e.g. for visitors, for showing at the flower show, to be made into jam etc. Try to follow the pattern that the poet has used – and don't use more than 30 words! (See children's work on p. 11.)

Creative Activities:

1. Look at the colour of oranges, lemons, grapefruit. Put orange trees, lemon trees and the sun into one picture, trying to make the fruit and the sunshine each brighter than the other. (See display photograph p. 11.)

Fruit & Vegetables

2. Visit the supermarket. (See Visits.) Look at the colour and shape of tomatoes, lemons, apples, pears, red and green peppers. See how they are piled on top of one another. (See 'Greengrocer' by John Cotton.) Look at cans of fruit and tins of soup. Look at jars of jam. See how the tins and jars are piled into castles.
   - Paint a pattern picture of lots of tomatoes, oranges, lemons, pears or red peppers. A group of children can work on this together. Cut out individual oranges and lemons etc. when they are dry. Paste in 'heaps' one on top of the other.
   - Paint a pattern picture of piled-up cans of soup, or jars of jam.
   - Paint a shop window with displays of fruit in cans and jars. (See John Cotton's 'Greengrocer'.) Think of the rounded shapes of fruit alternating with the straight-sided cans and jars.
   - Make a pattern of green apples. Mix different greens. Add a 'Buy our fresh apples' poster beside the apple pattern and use as a poster for shopping activities. (See display photo, p. 11.)
3. 'Tale of a Turnip'.
   - Make glove puppets, or puppets on a stick (old rulers are useful), for the characters in the story.
   - Make masks from cereal packets for children acting out the story.

   - A group can make a collage of the story with characters cut out and pasted on a frieze.
4. Make a collage of vegetables piled up haphazardly into a cut-out box or barrow. Use corrugated paper splashed with paint for marrows, wet-look plastic for peppers, green tissue paper frilled and curled round a pencil for parsley, sugar paper covered with old tights for potatoes etc.

Movement and Drama:

1. Make upward and outward growing movements slowly. Quickly curl back inside onion/bulb/seed. Alternate stretching and curling movements. Show with your body how roots reach down into the soil (see Classroom Activities, Vegetables No. 10) – in dry soil, in stony ground. In groups, show the movements of worms and grubs squirming round the roots of vegetables.
2. Make a fruit or vegetable stall with papier mâché fruit and vegetables. Think of the noise and bustle round the stalls in an open-air market. Imagine that you are a stall-holder trying to sell your wares. Imagine that you are a mother or father buying vegetables for the family. Get into an argument with the stall-holders.

Creatures of the Garden

Dragonfly

I am a small iridescent twig,
Silver wrapped like a thin sweet.
A catch-sun, though you will not catch me.
Too quick as I skim the waters I came from.
When I pause on a reed or a lily's landing pad
I'm watching you as you marvel.
You look again: I've gone!

John Cotton

Snails

After the rain,
when everything smells deep and green,
a hundred snails

go up and down our path, across the lawns
and sidewise on the garden wall
and back again.

Under their brown curled
shells, soft little horns
feel out for where they're going.

Where they have been,
these shining trails
catch in the grey light

like metal roads across a magic world.

Tony Charles

Insects

The ants rush around
from lawn to nest
they never pause
to have a rest

The spiders cast webs
from flower to bush
they are never seen working
or in a rush

The dragonflies hover
fast and slow
they never seem sure
of which way to go

The gardener watches
and wonders why
they never stop
to look at the sky

J. Walsh

daddy long legs
I'm sorry for you

you've got the wrong legs
for standing up

keep flying
and flopping

then you sail away
like a bony cloud

away across the field
to do it again

somewhere else

daddy long legs
wants to dance
but can't

his legs
are too weak

but he keeps
on trying

jump
    flop
jump
    flop
all over

Geoffrey Holloway

golden-growing on the hill

gorse bushes growing
green and tangly
thick and humpy
on the hill

gorse flowers growing
gold and gleamy
bright and sunny
on the bush
warm and still

gorse thorns growing
strong and hooky
sharp and scratchy
walls that will
keep safe
all small creatures
hiding under the
golden-flowering gorse
growing green and tangly
thick and humpy
gold and gleamy
bright and sunny
strong and hooky
sharp and scratchy
growing
on the hill.

Joan Poulson

Creatures of the Garden

Discussion and Observation:

- Name and discuss those who work under the earth (e.g. miners). Can you think of any others?
- Talk about those whose jobs require them to dig into the earth (gardeners, road repairmen, builders). Find others. Discuss what the conditions might be like.
- Talk about the child's own experience of making mud pies or helping in the garden.
- Name and talk about creatures who live under the earth.
- Name and talk about the creatures who visit our gardens. Look at pictures of familiar insects, animals and birds. Use information books from the library.
- Discuss how more creatures (butterflies, bees, birds) might be encouraged to come back to our gardens.
- Talk about wild gardens and conservation. Consider setting up a wild garden in a corner of the school playground.

Visits:

- Visit a conservation area. Talk to the volunteers. Take part in the conservation games which the Wildlife Trust runs in various centres in the summer term.

Classroom Activities:

1. Ask a group of children to dig up some earth on a trowel. Spread the soil over a large flat glass dish. Look at it from the top, then underneath. Use a magnifying glass.
2. Look at the colour of the earth. Look at the particles which make it up. Look at the shapes into which it spreads.
3. Look for living creatures in the soil. Watch their movements.
4. Feel the texture of the earth. Is it warm/dry/damp? Does it run easily through the fingers or is it damp and sticky? Does it break up finely or go into lumps? Try to find sandy soil/chalky soil/heavy clay and compare colour and texture.
5. Experiment with earth baked hard by the sun, then with wet soil taken from the same place on a rainy day.
6. Children can turn over a stone on the soil. Look for little creatures living beneath. Use a magnifying glass. Look for colour/shape/ movements of the creatures. Look for legs and feelers. Touch them carefully and see what happens. Return them to their environment when you have finished observing them.
7. The children might want to build a mini-zoo out of a clean glass jar or a plastic container for the creatures found under the stone. Put a thin layer of damp soil and some pebbles in the container. Keep the mini-zoo away from direct sunlight. Spray with water. RELEASE THE CREATURES AT THE END OF THE SCHOOL DAY.

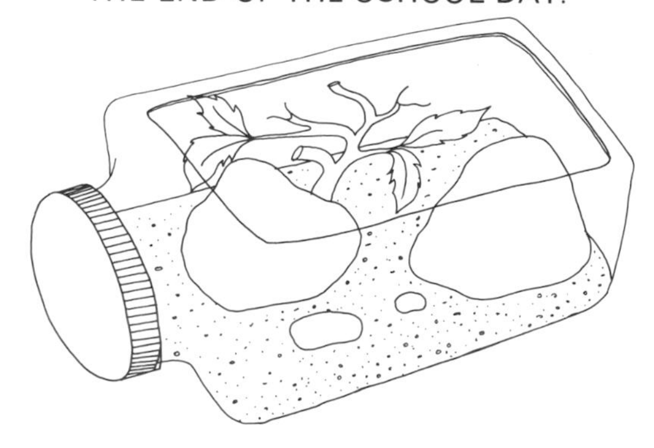

Creatures of the Garden

8. Children can collect some earthworms. Put them on a glass plate. Watch them move. Look at length/thickness/colour. Put one on a piece of drawing paper and listen to it move. Those who want to might touch and handle the worms. RETURN THE WORMS TO THE GARDEN AS SOON AS POSSIBLE. Talk about how they find their way about underground. Talk about other creatures who rely to a great extent on touch, smell and sound.

9. Let groups of children mark out a section of the school field with string into half metre squares. Using a magnifying glass, clip-board and pencils, they could note down everything that is growing or moving within their own particular square. Make sketches. Give the children ten minutes to complete the exercise.

   Enlarge the grid on the classroom wall, and make notes and sketches of all the plant and insect life in that part of the field. (This is one way in which researchers work.)

10. Experiment with a Pandora's box. (Use a crisp carton with holes cut out for wrists.) A selection of different objects should be hidden, one at a time (e.g. a feather, a wet sponge, a lemon, a nail brush). The child can feel each object and find words to describe its texture and use. Make this a guessing game. (See Language Activities.)

11. It may be possible to build a simple bird table near the classroom window. Put out fruit, breadcrumbs, water and wild bird seed. Look at the shape/size/colour of the visiting birds. Try to identify regular visitors. Make a bird count. (See Snow, Classroom Activities, No. 5.)

Language Activities:

1. You have worked with the Pandora's box (see above). Now try out some blindfold games in the classroom. Have you ever hidden away under the bed, or in a dark cupboard, or in the garden shed? Tell about how you feel playing a game where you are blindfolded, or where you hide away in a dark place for a short time and must rely on your sense of touch. Have you ever hidden away from your parents for a time? Tell how you felt as they called your name.

Creatures of the Garden

2. Tell about waking up in the middle of the night, when all the lights are out, and finding your way to the bathroom/downstairs to the kitchen/to your parents' bedroom – without switching on the light.
3. Look at the inhabitants of your mini-zoo through a magnifying glass. If, like Alice in Wonderland, you became very, very small, do you think that some of these tiny creatures might look like fierce dragons? Imagine an encounter with an enormous earwig dragon or a beetle dragon, or a dragonfly as big as Concorde. (See John Cotton's 'Dragonfly'.) Describe the look and the sound of the huge beast. Tell what happens.
4. Ask permission to dig a hole in the garden or in some waste ground – not in the park! Look at the colour of the earth. Feel the particles of soil. You may find some broken toys, some rusty nails, an old penny – you might even find some bones! Write about finding buried treasure.
5. Listen to 'Snails' by Tony Charles.

   'Where they have been
   these shining trails
   catch in the grey light
   like metal roads across a
   magic world'

   Tony Charles has looked very carefully at what snails do and how they move. Choose another creature which you have found in the garden. Watch its movements and try to write about it with the acute observation and the hint of magic that this poet has used. Where might the snails' metal roads lead to?
6. Listen to John Cotton's 'Dragonfly'. In this poem he pretends to speak as a dragonfly himself. He describes himself as 'Silver wrapped like a thin sweet'. Choose another insect or underground creature that you have examined, and try to put yourself into its skin. Find something ordinary to which you can compare your creature, but don't name it. (Rather like writing a riddle.) Begin, for example, by saying 'I am a loop of knicker elastic', and go on to describe your movements and looks as a worm. Or try 'I am striped and fat as a humbug' (bumble bee); or use Geoffrey Holloway's image for daddy-long-legs, 'I am a bony cloud'. Once you get the idea of image it is easy. This is one of the ways a poet captures the attention of the reader.
7. Listen to Joan Poulson's 'golden-growing on the hill'. Listen carefully to the way in which she describes the gorse bushes so that you can almost see and feel them. Look for the rhythmic words which make this poem sound like a song, e.g. 'green and tangly', 'gold and gleamy'. Can you look for movement words which might make a song about caterpillars/worms/spiders/beetles in the same kind of way. (See Movement and Drama.)
8. Think of a garden you know. Tell about watching for the first green shoots. Tell how you would encourage bees and butterflies to come to your garden. Make up a 'brochure' (rather like a holiday booklet from a travel agent) and address it to the insects, setting out the delights of your conservation garden. Put in lots of illustrations and make it very colourful.
9. Look at all the creatures you can find in the garden and make a list of them. (This is what five-year-old David Blair has done in his piece of writing. See photo next page.) The next step would be to take the things on the list, chop up the lines and put into the form of a poem. He did not want to do this, and the writing makes sense just as it is. Choose to put your

Creatures of the Garden

list of garden creatures either into a prose piece (like David's) or into a list poem. Use your eyes and ears to help you. J. Walsh has put his list of insects into a poem. (See 'Insects' by J. Walsh.)

Creative Activities:

1. Using wet paper, paint tall 'green and tangly, strong and hooky' grasses, gorse, thistles, etc. as a group project. (See display photo, p. 17.)

   Another group can draw snails, butterflies, caterpillrs, dragonflies, beetles etc. in felt-tip pen. Cut these creatures out and glue onto the wild garden background when it is dry. Fill as much of the paper as possible to get the best effect.

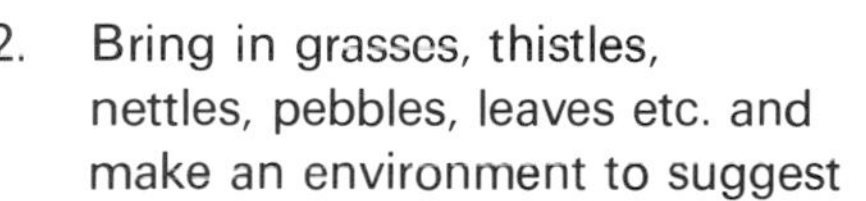

2. Bring in grasses, thistles, nettles, pebbles, leaves etc. and make an environment to suggest the scene at a garden creature's level – a worm's eye view! Model worms, beetles, hedgehogs etc. from clay or modelling dough. Bake and paint. Arrange the finished creatures in their own 'real' environment.

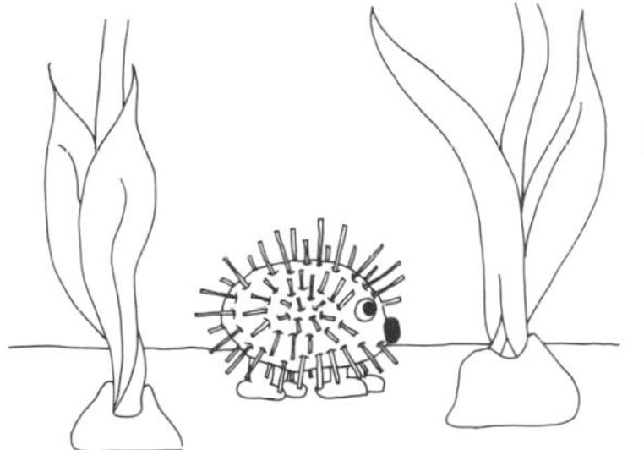

Drama and Movement:

1. Read Joan Poulson's poem 'golden-growing on the hill'. With your fingers, knees and elbows, make yourself 'strong and hooky, sharp and scratchy' etc. Let half the class be the gorse and the others the small creatures hiding and exploring. Change places.
2. Read Geoffrey Holloway's 'daddy-long-legs'. Make your legs as long and floppy as you can. Try to stand and dance with 'the wrong legs'. Make your dance as funny as you can. Find a tape, or make up music to go with your daddy-long-legs dance. Make yourself into 'a bony cloud'.

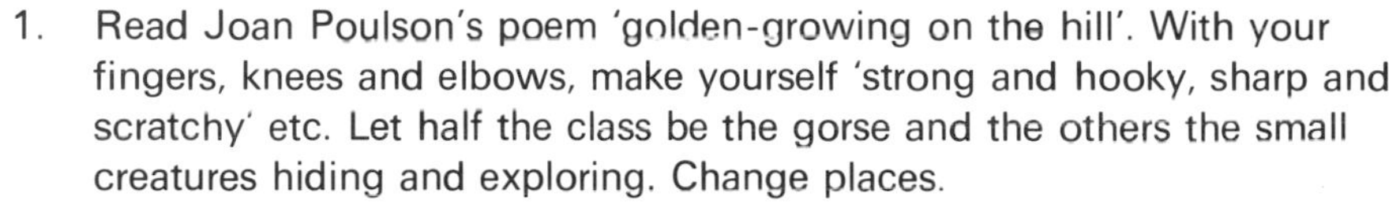

3. As creatures explore their environment, each will move in a different kind of way. You have watched those found beneath a stone, you have watched spiders, butterflies and worms. Find words to express the movement of these creatures. Now show, first with your fingers, hands and arms, then with your whole body, how these different creatures might move.

   Work together at first, then divide into groups. Move in as many different ways as possible, showing how different creatures might explore their environment.

Colour

Mid-summer Feast

Serve a slice of sunshine
Pass the plate of breeze,
Garnish with a rainbow
As vivid as you please.

RED of oriental poppy
YELLOW of the flag
ORANGE of fiery marigold
BLUE sea-holly's jag
GREEN of summer grass
INDIGO's iris frill
VIOLET cat-faced pansies
Mix them as you will.

Sip the wine of morning dew,
Wash down with gentle rain,
Try a spoon of ice-cool cloud
Before the day hots up again.

Moira Andrew

The Garden

What can you see in the garden?
What can you see in the grass?
There are patches of buttercup yellow
that powder your feet as you pass.
There are daises with petals that open
and close with the coming of night,
and bird's eye, as blue as the sky is,
and convolvulus, rosy . . . or white.

The field is awash with sweet clover
and noisy with hundreds of bees;
there are violets deep in the ditches,
and aconites under the trees . . .
There are poppies as red as a post box
and thistle and dandelion too.
Did ever you see such a garden?
An artist should paint it.
Could you?

Jean Kenward

The paint box

'Cobalt and umber and ultramarine,
Ivory, black and emerald green –
What shall I paint to give pleasure to you?'
'Paint for me something utterly new.'

'I have painted you tigers in crimson and white.'
'The colours were good and you painted aright.'
'I have painted a cock and a camel in blue.
And a panther in purple.' 'You painted them true.

Now mix me a colour that nobody knows,
And paint me a country where nobody goes,
And put in people a little like you,
Watching a unicorn drinking the dew.'

E. V. Rieu

Seed Songs

The sunflower
sings the hours in
when yellow summer
days begin.

Flighty poppies,
blown on air
sing of scarlet
clothes to wear.

The sycamore sings,
I'll be a tree
the high blue sky
will cover me;

While in the orchard
last year's plum
sings green, green, green
as he splits his stone.

Irene Rawnsley

Cornflowers

fade
from the outside
in

dozens
of dusty
white mouths
on pale
blue throats

tiny
purple tips
on
curved black stamens.

Patricia Pogson

Primary

A pair of goldfinches
dip across the lawn.

One clips two
forget-me-nots.

I imagine a blue nest
exuberant with yellow and red

Patricia Pogson

Colour

Discussion and Observation:

- Name and collect examples of different colours, eg from paint colour charts.
- Make a colour display in the classroom. Make a graph of favourite colours.
- Talk about colours in the classroom: books, toys, clothes, paints.
- Learn how to make new colours by mixing paint, layering tissue paper, stroking oil-based pastels one colour on top of another, and using wax resist techniques.
- Bring a few flowers into school. Look at the colours of stem, leaves, petals. Find words to describe the varying colours. (Use paint charts or Roget's Thesaurus.) Make up new colour words. (See children's work on p. 13.)
- Look at the undersides of leaves and petals. Do the colours look the same?
- Look at how flowers fade and the way colours change. (See 'Cornflowers' by Patricia Pogson.)

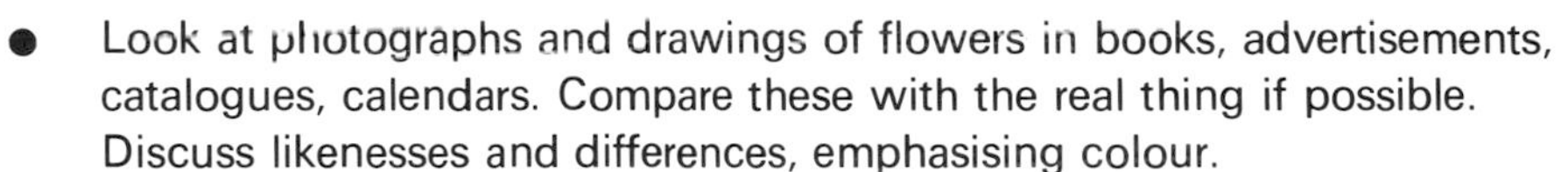

- Look at photographs and drawings of flowers in books, advertisements, catalogues, calendars. Compare these with the real thing if possible. Discuss likenesses and differences, emphasising colour.
- Talk about the world without colour, for example at night, the garden in winter, in a cave, inside a cupboard.

Visits:

- Visit the local park, or an open garden in high summer. Look at the variety of vivid colours. Look for white flowers, and see how many different whites you can find (from creamy roses to snowy gypsophila).
- Visit the shops selling flowers. Look at the way the flowers are grouped in bunches to attract passers-by.
- Visit the nearest meadow, nature trail or common. Look at the way some flowers hide their colour (dog-violets) and others blaze their presence (gorse bushes, red campion). Why do you think this happens?

Classroom Activities:

1. Make a graph of favourite colours.
2. Make a class/group/individual book about colour, using as many different colour words as you can find – or make them up.
3. Look at all the colours in the paintbox. Paint a picture using shades of one colour. (See Creative Activities.) Mix paints and experiment with colour. Overlay coloured tissue paper or cellophane – blue/yellow, yellow/red, red/blue. This can be done very effectively on the window, and may be developed to give a stained glass effect.

Colour

4. Collect scraps of material – shades of one colour in different textures.
5. Set up table-top displays of colour using background drapes, glass, flowers, books, paint-pots etc. (See display, p. 21.)
6. Think of one special colour. Try – Hiding under a green bush
   Walking under a red/blue/green umbrella
   Making cellophane-covered 'hiding boxes'
   (See Language Activities, No. 2)
   Looking at the world through sunglasses
7. Bring flowers into school. Look at the colours of the flowers. Smell the perfume. Feel the texture of stem, leaves, petals.
8. Look at the colours in the greengrocer's window or in the vegetable patch.
9. Look at different greens in the garden, field or park.
10. Make a class/group/individual book about flowers.
11. Make up detergent bubbles. Look at the colour and shape. Touch the bubbles and listen to them pop.
12. At home, switch off the light and stand in the dark. Look and listen. How does it feel?
13. Look out of the window on the way to bed. Colours have disappeared. See how shadows and movements can be seen as eyes become used to the darkness. Is it really a world without colour? Look at night-time photographs and pictures.

Language Activities:

1. Mixing Colours. What happens when you mix blue and yellow? red and blue? yellow and red? Add more of one colour than another. What has happened? Can you give your new colour a name? (Read 'The paint box' by E. V. Rieu . . . 'Now mix me a colour that nobody knows. . .')
2. Make a miniature 'hiding box'. Take a shoe box and cut a hole in the lid. Cover the hole with coloured cellophane. Build a miniature world inside the box, e.g. space station, the woods at night, a summer garden, an underwater pool. Make a 'spy hole' in the end of the box. Name your coloured world. Write a travelogue about your new world.

3. Think about what makes a colour as it is. Make a list of all the things you can think of that are *always* blue/green/red/yellow and make a poem from the list. You can use a question as a title, for example 'What is blue?'
4. Read Patricia Pogson's 'Primary'. She has written a poem using the three primary colours, red, blue and yellow. See if you can bring three colours into one poem. You might begin 'A pair of blackbirds. . .' or 'Two robin redbreasts. . .'. Let them fly into the garden and touch a flower. What might happen to the petals? What happens next?
5. Look at the garden on a summer's day. Listen to the insects. Smell the perfume. Read Jean Kenward's poem 'The Garden'. Try to build a poem using all the sights and sounds and smells of your garden.

Colour

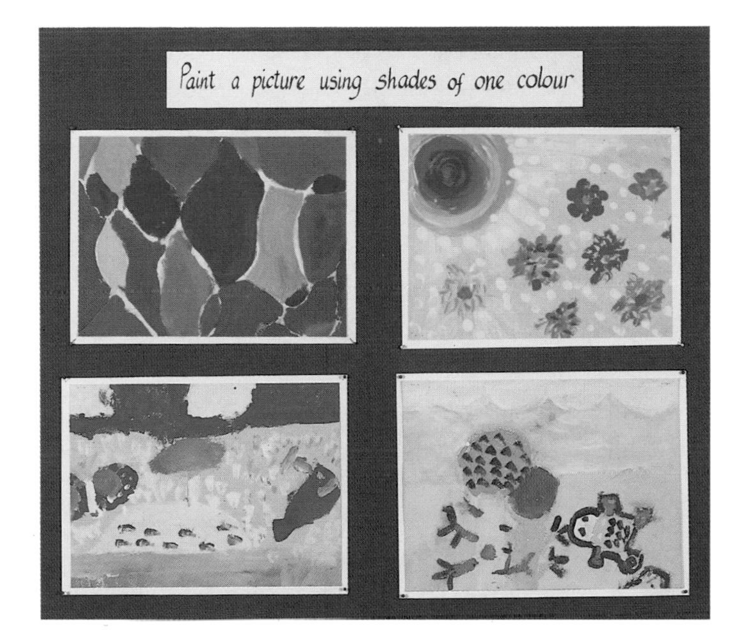

6. Find out the colours of the rainbow. Make a poem using all the colours in the correct sequence. Think of the pot of gold that is supposed to be at the end of the rainbow. Write about finding the pot of gold. What would you do with it? (Read 'Mid-summer Feast'.)

Creative Activities:

1. Paint a picture using shades of one colour. It can be a pattern picture, a picture of a wood with trees and bushes, all in shades of green. Put in a green frog hiding under green leaves in the long green grass. Make a blue underwater picture with fish and rocks and seaweed all in shades of blue. (See photograph above.)
2. Paint a picture using red, yellow and blue. See what happens. Read Patricia Pogson's 'Primary'. Paint a picture for her poem. (See Language Activities.)
3. Bring in a large yellow flower or a bunch of marigolds. Put the yellow flower (or the marigolds) and the sun into one painting, trying to make each brighter than the other.
4. Paint a summer garden. Paint large flowers. Think of round shapes (pansies, roses), bell shapes (foxgloves, nasturtiums), mop-head shapes with lots of petals on each flower (marigolds, moon-daisies). Use red, yellow and blue for the flowers. Paint lots of flowers, one on top of the other. Fill the paper. (See Jean Kenward's 'The Garden'.)

Colour

5. Make an orange-red fiery picture on wet paper. Use spiky, wobbly shapes and all the hot colours. Make a cool blue picture using smooth curved lines.
6. Experiment with coloured cellophane and tissue paper to make overlapping patterns/flower shapes on the window. Try for a stained glass effect.
7. Make large multi-petalled flowers using different kinds of paper – typing paper, tissue paper, gummed paper. Cut or tear the petals. Use shades of yellow through to orange, e.g. sunflowers and marigolds, or shades of pink through red to purple, e.g. peonies.
8. Make a large group panel – 'The Enchanted Forest' – with all kinds of tree shapes cut or torn from tissue paper. Use a pale coloured background to let the light through. Use the tissue paper flat and transparent, so that you get an overlapping effect. Invent strange magic animals to put into the enchanted forest. (See 'The paint box': 'I have painted a cock and a camel in blue, and a panther in purple.' 'You painted them true.')

9. Make blow-pattern pictures using thick paint and a straw. Can you see flower shapes, tree shapes, bird or animal shapes, in your picture? Look for funny shapes and frightening shapes.

Movement and Drama:

1. Choose a colour and move as you think the colour would move. Would blue be slow and smooth? Would red be spiky and fiery?
2. Look at your own blow-pattern. Decide how your pattern might move. Take a partner and see if you can make up a dance from your blow-pictures.
3. Listen to Jean Kenward's 'The Garden' – 'There are daisies with petals that open/and close with the coming of night'. Make opening and closing movements. Use all your body and work very slowly. Stretch outwards and upwards for the morning movements. Curl back into your fingertips for night-time.
4. Listen to Patricia Pogson's 'Cornflowers'. Use your body to grow like the cornflower, then 'fade/from the outside in'. Use every part of your body and leave only 'tiny/purple tips/on/curved black stamens'.
5. Make a rainbow sequence so that seven people each have a different colour to represent. Read 'Mid-summer Feast', and make one movement slide into the next. You might make up a music sequence to go with your rainbow dance.
6. Blow detergent bubbles. Watch how they float. Look at the shapes. Move in twos and threes like bubbles floating across the sky.
7. Read Irene Rawnsley's 'Seed Songs'. Make up music to fit the songs. How would a sunflower sing? What kind of music would poppies make? Try foxgloves, forget-me-nots, night-scented stocks. Make up new songs for other flowers in the garden.

Sea and Shore

The sea

The sea can be angry.
The sea can be rough.
The sea can be vicious.
The sea can be tough.

The sea can rip.
The sea can tear.
The sea can roar
Like a hungry bear.

The sea can be gentle.
The sea can be flat.
The sea can be calm
As a sleeping cat.

The sea can glide
Over the sand
Stroking the beach
Like a giant hand.

John Foster

Sea seasons

The sea bounces
over barnacles,
bobbing and buckling
in the springtime breeze.

The sea slithers
across shingle,
splintering and sparkling
under a bright summer sun.

The sea prowls
over pebbles,
pimpling and prickling
on damp autumn days.

The sea rushes
across rocks
ranting and raving
when winter winds blow.

Moira Andrew

Wave

I am one of an endless family,
My brothers and sisters
Never far behind.
I crash and I swirl,
Grind pebbles, growl,
And gnaw the bones of the land
Like a great wet dog.

John Cotton

Exploring the rock pool

We explore the rock pool
A small world of its own:
The scuttling crab, quick shrimps,
Sea polished stone
With hints of colours
Enhanced by the light –

Refracting water
Making all so bright.
The strands of seaweed
Verdant, sleek as silk,
The tiny limpets,
Shells as white as milk.
A sea in miniature
Which lasts just for a day,
When the tide renews it
Washing the old away.

John Cotton

Winter Gulls

Watch them!
  Watch the seagulls
sweeping
  through the air
crying
  while they wheel away,
dipping
  as you stare . . .
climbing into
  sky-blue
distances,
  and then
plunging swiftly
  downwards
till they rise
  again.

Toss your bits
  of bread up
higher –
  higher still.
Will they –
  will they catch them?
Yes! I guess
  they will!
Hear the winter
  seagulls
screaming
  as they go,
emptiness
  above them,
and the sea
  below!

Jean Kenward

Sea and Shore

Visits: The most successful observation and discussion will arise from a visit to the seaside, but many children will, of course, already have some direct experience of the sea from holidays with their families. If you organise a visit to the seaside for the children, set them up before you go to use their senses, looking, listening, smelling, touching, so that they not only enjoy themselves but gain as much as possible from the experience.

Visit a maritime museum, or a lifeboat station.

Discussion and Observation

- Look at the waves, the pattern they make in different kinds of weather, the patterns they leave behind on the sand.
- Look at the movement of the waves, how different in summer and winter, how different when the wind is quiet and in a storm. (See John Foster's 'The Sea' and Moira Andrew's 'Sea seasons'.)
- Look at the movement of gulls. (See Jean Kenward's 'Winter Gulls'.)
- Explore a rock pool. Look for all the different kinds of fish, stones, weed, that you can find. Try to identify them. (See John Cotton's poem, 'Exploring the rock pool'.)
- Listen to the sound of gulls, to the waves, to children's voices. Hold a shell to your ear and listen to the sound of the sea.
- Touch the sand. Let dry sand trickle through your fingers. Compare it with wet sand. Build a sand castle.
- Feel the difference: sand on a hot afternoon, and on a cold winter's day.
- Feel the difference in temperature between sea water and the water in a rock pool. Enjoy splashing or swimming in the sea. TAKE GREAT CARE – THE SEA CAN BE DANGEROUS. Enjoy the feeling of your whole body in the waves. Can you float?
- Taste sea water on the tip of your tongue. Can you taste the salt?
- Find some interesting flotsam and bring it back to school. Where do you think it might have come from?

Classroom Activities:

1. In the sand tray feel the difference between dry and wet sand. Find funnels and sieves that dry sand will run through. Wet the sand a little at a time, and find out what texture is best for building a sand castle. Have a sand castle competition. You will need lots of shells, paper flags, twigs, pebbles etc. Decide who should live in your castle.
2. Read John Cotton's 'Exploring the rock pool'. When you visit the seaside spend some time looking closely in a rock pool. Note all the creatures, pebbles and weed that you can see. When you get back to school, make a grid (perhaps with the pool shape outlined in blue pencil), and mark down the names and shapes of everything you saw. Mark living creatures in black, weed and other plants in green, and pebbles etc. in brown. Note size and shape. Now compare your grid with that of others in the class and find out which pools had most life in them.
3. Read Jean Kenward's 'Winter Gulls'. From a nature book see how many different kinds of gull you can identify. Make a class nature book about seagulls.
4. Did you find any interesting flotsam on the shore-line? (See Visits.) Make a sculpture using some of the bits and pieces you found. Make your finished shape as unusual as you can. It need not represent anything, but simply be a satisfactory shape. Find a name for your sculpture and hold an exhibition.

Sea and Shore

5. Fill the water trough. It is best to take it outside if the weather is suitable. Find some things which you think will float, and others which will sink. Test them out. Now make a chart showing floating and sinking.

   Draw a line across the middle of the page. Draw and name all those things which sink beneath the line, and those which float just above the line.

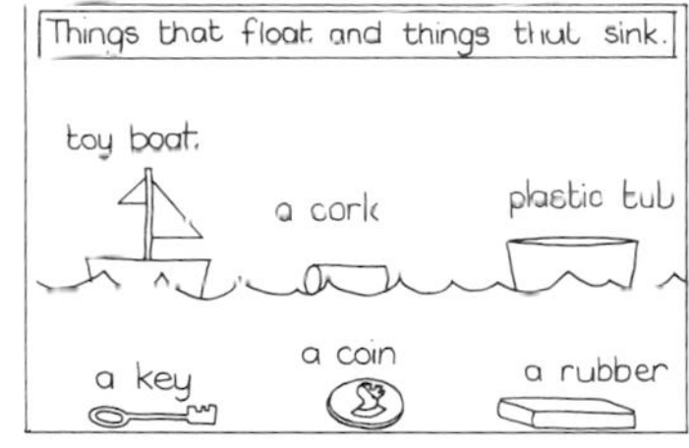

6. Again using the water trough, try making waves using as many wave-making ideas as you can. Don't use your hands. See who can design the best wave-making invention. Put your design on paper so that someone else can follow the instructions for making it. (Read John Cotton's 'Wave'.)

Language Activities:

1. Read John Cotton's poem 'Wave'. Look and listen to the waves. Make a list of all the sound and movement words you can find to describe waves. Then put yourself in place of the sea and begin your poem with 'I can/am/like . . .' and tell what sounds and movements you can make. Your poem will be in the form of a riddle, so you might want to end it with the question 'What am I?'
2. Read Moira Andrew's 'Sea seasons'. This poem is written in the sequence of the four seasons, and is an easy form to copy. Try a different kind of sequence poem using the days of the week, the alphabet or morning through to night. Then take a tree/the wind/a river as it might look through the seasons of the year.
3. Explore a rock pool, just as a scientist might. (See Discussion and Observation.) Look at the list of creatures you have found. Now put all your finds together into a list poem. Watch the rhythms as you read over

Sea and Shore

your lines, and this will help you put your ideas into the best order. (Read John Cotton's poem 'Exploring the rock pool'.)

4. Watch the movement of birds. Find words to describe these movements and print them neatly on a bird-shaped mobile and hang it up in the classroom so that it moves in the breeze. You need to use both sides for your words.

   Work as a group and see how many interesting words you can find. Now read Jean Kenward's poem 'Winter Gulls' and note some of the excellent words she has used '. . . sweeping, dipping, plunging'. Add these words if you haven't already used them. Try putting them together as a song. Make up sea music on percussion instruments.

5. Look at the first two verses of John Foster's poem, 'The sea'. He reminds us that the sea can be 'angry/rough/vicious/tough', that it can 'rip/tear/roar'. Think of those who make their living on or near the sea; fishermen, sailors, lifeboatmen etc. Think of the story you could tell if you were caught in a storm at sea. Tell your story to a reporter from television or a newspaper. Make it as vivid as you can. Tell all you saw and heard, all you felt or imagined, how happy you were to be home.

Creative Activities:

1. See John Cotton's poem, 'Wave'. Look at the pattern made by the waves. (See Visits and Classroom Activities.) Take a piece of sugar paper and lay some string out in wave patterns. Tack the ends with a dab of glue. Now, using a straw, blow paint over the string. When it is dry, remove the string very carefully and you will be left with wave patterns in white relief. (This can be also be done as a wax resist pattern, see photo p. 29.)
2. Using blues and greens, mix paint on the page and make an all-over sea picture, so that it shows lights and depths. Then cut out rounded boulder shapes in browns and greens and greys. Make stones and pebbles, so that you have a whole range of sizes and colours. When your painted seascape is dry, paste the stone-shapes on to your picture to make a pebbled shoreline, overlapping the shapes to crowd the picture, making the shore deep with stones.
3. Look at seagulls. Read Jean Kenward's poem, 'Winter Gulls'. Make bird mobiles, and 'fly' them at different levels from a cord across the classroom. Remember to have some of the birds 'sweeping/dipping/climbing' and make the cut-out shapes follow these different movements. Consult your bird books for help if necessary.
4. Read Moira Andrew's 'Sea seasons'. Take a fairly large sheet of paper and divide it into four sections. Use oil-based crayons to show trees/a meadow/shore in spring, summer, autumn, winter.
5. Read John Cotton's 'Exploring the rock pool'. Look carefully at the shapes and colours of everything you have found in a rock pool when you visited the shore. (See Visits.) Assemble as many different sea-creatures as you can, using paint, cut-outs in foil, newspaper, doily lace, tissue paper etc. Place in overlapping positions within a blue line (representing the rock pool). Now cover over in cellophane in a mixture of blues and greens.

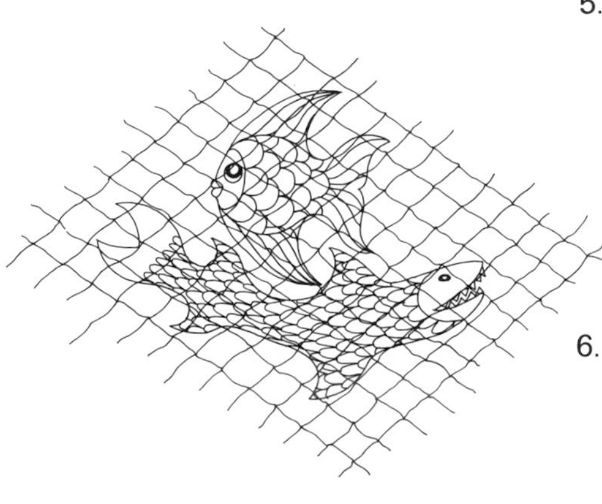

6. Look at pictures of fish. Draw fish outlines in white wax crayon. Make elaborate scale patterns on the side of the fish. Wash over with blue/green paint to make a wax resist.

Sea and Shore

Wax resist wave pattern, creative activities, no. 1

7. Again take the fish motif, but this time cut out the fish shapes and decorate in overlapping tissue paper and foil to make the scales. Make the pattern look very colourful and exciting. Work as a group. Paste the fish on a background, all jostling with one another. Cover with netting to look like a very vivid fisherman's catch.

Movement and Drama:

1. Read Jean Kenward's poem 'Winter Gulls'. Listen to the movement words she has used. Add more of your own. (See Language Activities.) Now use your whole body to 'sweep/dip/climb/plunge', making large movements across the hall floor. It may be possible to find suitable sea music to make these winter gull movements into a dance. Would the same movements be suitable for nesting time? night time? feeding time? Find other movements to fit these activities.
2. Look at the movements of waves. Read John Cotton's poem 'Wave'. He says that waves are 'one of an endless family'. Join hands in twos and threes and make undulating movements, one person dipping down as another rises, just as the sea does. Show how you can 'bounce/slither/prowl/rush' as in Moira Andrew's 'Sea seasons'.
3. Visit a lifeboat station. Watch how the men practise answering a distress call. Make this into a short drama, taking care to keep to the correct sequence of events.

The Docks and Harbour

Breakfast in the Harbour

Early morning sunshine
Bounces over wavetips,
Ricochets from bridges,
Tinsel points the day.

Swans patrol the moorings,
Ploughing up reflections.
Yachtsmen, waking slowly,
Sip steaming mugs of tea.

In the centre of the harbour
A screeching yowl announces
That the dredger is awake
And starting a new day.

Gulping slime in bucketfuls
It's cleaning out a channel,
Slurping up the mud and silt
And taking it away.

A liner at the entrance
Waits for a clearer passage.
Tugs hoot a greeting
As they leave.

A flock of gulls, alerted
To the chance of fresh-dug titbits,
Fly in with loud, demanding cries,
And circle, eagerly.

Edna Eglinton

The Harbour

Boats are bobbling
under the hill.
They're safe in the harbour
but they won't keep still.

They're all of a fidget,
They long to go
out on the great big
ocean's flow.

They don't like dozing
half asleep
when the far seas beckon,
fathoms deep.

You can hear them whisper
each to each:
We're tired of pebbles,
and a sandy beach. . .

But the old ones answer
Hush! Keep still!
It's safe in harbour
under the hill.

Jean Kenward

Pictures from a Harbour

1
Vessels loll alongside quays
butting motor tyres or fenders
of hemp against the concrete
walls.

2
Rope and chain twang from ship
to shore like the strings
of a giant guitar playing on
air.

3
Cranes circle, raise and lower
nets of cargo from black holds,
lift, in a heavy dance, vast deck
containers.

4
In the harbour everything is bulk
and moves to the repeating tide
that feeds ships in and out of exotic
ports.

John Fairfax

The harbour wall

In winter,
when the wind blows wild,
the sea's as grey
as a muddy puddle.

Then the harbour wall
curls its long arm
around the boats
bobbing in a huddle.

I'll keep you safe,
the wall seems to say,
come here. And it gives
the boats a cuddle.

Wes Magee

Strikebound

The ship's side gapes,
its unhealed wound still bare;
no caulker's tool
is spitting compressed air.
Where rustblood drips
from yet unplated frames
no pyrotechnic
welders sign their names.

A crane hook yawns
as with the wind it sways
and, metronomic,
whiles away its days.

Maurice Rutherford

The Docks and Harbour

Visits: It would be ideal if the children were able to visit the docks, sea wall or harbour. Best of all would be a visit to a busy fishing harbour.

- Watch a catch being unloaded. Visit the fish market.
- Watch what happens at the docks. Are they still in use, or have they been converted to leisure activities?
- Walk along the sea-wall. What is its purpose?

If you are unable to make such visits, use pictures, films, transparencies to get the effect.

Discussion and Observation:

- Look at the movements of boats. Watch the gulls swooping over fishing boats. Look at the movement of buoys, flags, bunting, floats, ropes, people.
- Look at the way fishermen/dockers are dressed.
- Look at the shape of cranes/boats/the harbour wall.
- Look at the way boxes are stacked/nets are dried/lobster pots are piled up/ropes are coiled.
- Look at the ships being loaded/unloaded at the docks. What cargoes do they carry? Watch the movement of cranes.
- Listen to the sound of gulls/water slapping the sides of boats/shouted instructions/engines.
- Listen to the sound of waves on the sea side of the harbour wall. Look at the movement of boats and sea on either side of the wall. Look for differences. Why should this happen?

The Docks and Harbour

- Touch the ice used for packing fish.
- Look for colour, e.g. oilskins/boats/floats/welding flames.
- Look for the patterns on the water. Does the weather make a difference?

Classroom Activities:

1. Talk about the safety that the harbour provides. See Jean Kenward's poem, 'It's safe in the harbour/under the hill.' Talk about the difference in the movement of the sea inside and beyond the harbour/sea wall.
2. Make paper boats and sail them in the classroom sink/the water tray/a puddle. Experiment with different kinds of materials to make boats, e.g. cork, card, balsa wood, twigs, polystyrene. See which boats do best. Can you think why?
3. Make a crane with string wound round a bobbin.

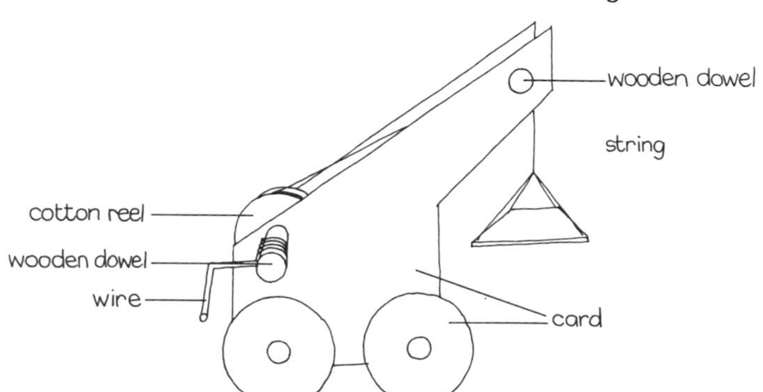

Experiment with pulleys to find out which is the best way to lift a load. Try paper clips/plasticine/counting bricks/buttons, as cargo.

(See 'Pictures from a Harbour' by John Fairfax.

'Cranes circle, raise and lower nets of cargo from black holds. . .')

4. Talk about the docks or the harbour nearest the school. Find out what is the most usual cargo/the most common kind of fish caught. Make a wall chart to display the results.
5. Experiment with things that float or sink. Make a floating and sinking chart.
6. Read Edna Eglinton's poem 'Breakfast in the Harbour'. She mentions three different kinds of boats/ships. See how many names and kinds of boats you can find, starting perhaps from ancient boats like coracle and kayak. Find out what each kind of boat is used for. Make a wall picture or class book showing what you have discovered.
7. Experiment with wave-making. If it is sunny, go outside with a bowl of water. Use a rolled-up newspaper to make waves in the water. Can you find a better way of making the water move? Invent a wave-making machine.

   Can you make a dam or a breakwater to keep one part of the water calm? Think of animals who build dams. Why do they do this?

Language Activities:

1. Imagine that you are about to make a journey by ship across the ocean. Tell or write how you would feel as you left the safety of the harbour to set out on your great adventure. Write a letter home to tell your parents what is happening, what sights you have seen, what discoveries you have made.
2. Read 'Pictures from a Harbour' by John Fairfax. In this poem he has put four short verses together describing things he sees around him. On your visit to the docks or harbour make notes of four different scenes. Stand in one place and turn in four different directions. Write down what you see and hear. You could make these notes into a picture poem. (See Creative Activities.)

The Docks and Harbour

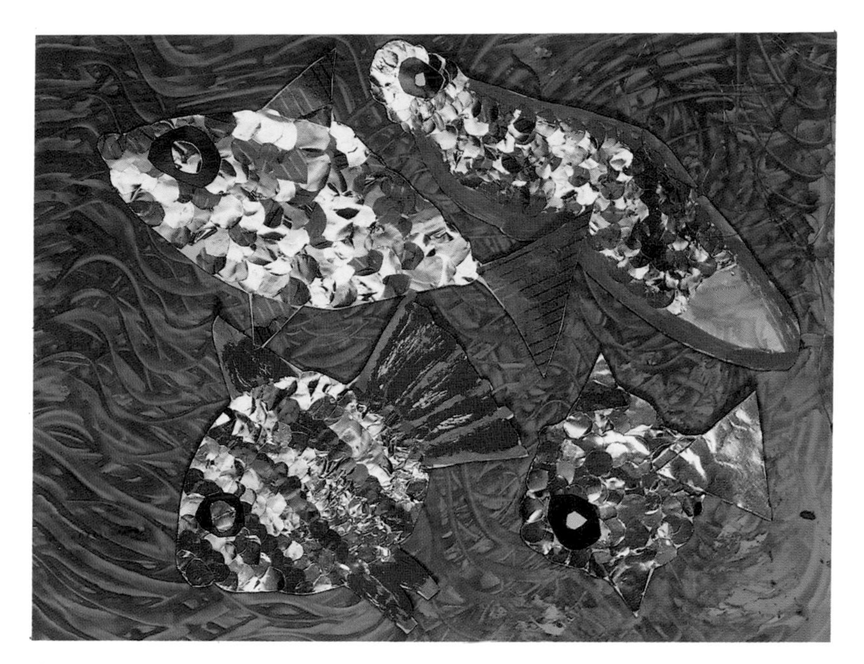

3. Read Maurice Rutherford's poem 'Strikebound'. This poem gives a bleak picture of a shipbuilder's yard during a strike when everything is quiet and still. Write a copy-cat poem picturing the shipyard at work, with all the noise and busy-ness, the colour and movement of the men, machines and tools on a working day.
4. Read Moira Andrew's poem, 'Newlyn Bay' (See title page). She has used shape to suggest the words 'tethered' and 'dancing'. When you have looked carefully at the movement of boats/floats/flags/buoys etc., write a short poem which gives a shape to movement words. Space letters out for words like 'waves', 'bobbing', 'floating'.
5. Look at the sea/harbour wall. Think of the safety which it provides, how different the sea is either side of the wall. (See Discussion and Observation.) Read Wes Magee's poem, 'The harbour wall'. He begins his poem with the words 'In winter . . .' Try a copy-cat poem beginning 'In spring . . .' 'In summer . . .' Then write another verse beginning 'In winter . . .' to show how different everything, sea/waves/weather/your clothes, would be when 'the wind blows wild'.
6. Look for all the movement words you can find to describe water/waves/boats. Make a list of them and use them to make a list poem beginning, e.g.

   'Boats
     bob
     dip
     curtsey
     fidget. . .'

   and so on for waves, water etc. Use the words in the poems first, then add others of your own. You could work as a group to write this poem.

Creative Activities:

1. As a group activity, cut out fairly large fish shapes. Make them as unusual as you can. Using coloured foil, with paint where necessary, make really colourful and imaginative fish with huge eyes, overlapping the scales, collage-fashion. Paste the fish on to a background of painted waves, and tack a length of netting over them to make it look as though they were caught in a fishing boat's net. (See photo above.)

The Docks and Harbour

2. Read Wes Magee's poem, 'The harbour wall'. Make a large wall frieze with the sea painted rough-looking with huge waves on one side, calm and flat on the other. Divide the picture by a curved harbour wall made from a collage of painted stones. Inside the wall, place painted boats 'bobbing in a huddle'; beyond the wall have boats pitching up and down on the waves. Make it clear that 'the harbour wall/curls its long arm/around the boats. . .' (See display photograph, p. 31.)
3. Following a visit to the docks or the harbour make a picture poem. (See Language Activities, No. 2). You should have notes on four scenes taken from one place. Paint a picture of the docks or harbour as you remember the scene – think of shape, colour, movement. Then put your four snapshot poems on the appropriate place on the picture, either writing directly on the surface or cutting out your poems and pasting them on.
4. Imagine that you are starting off on the adventure of a lifetime on a sailing ship. (See Language Activities.) Imagine that you have crossed the ocean. You have found an uninhabited island – perhaps there is treasure there.

Make a model of the island using papier mâché. Show the trees and plants, the hills and the shoreline. If you think that there might be treasure, give a clue as to where it might be found. Make a map of the island, just as sailors of old might have done.

5. Read Moira Andrew's poem 'Newlyn Bay' (on title page). Make a picture of a harbour at night, dark sky, dark sea, dark boats. When it is almost dry paint in the bright riding lights 'flickering/like fireflies/in the summer dark'. Make your lights as vivid as you can using clear clean paint.
6. Look at the waves. Watch the patterns they make inside and beyond the harbour wall. Make wave patterns using very thick paint on paper with a shiny surface. Make the patterns using either fingers (messy!) or a cardboard comb. Mix more colour on the paper, so that there is a deep-sea effect. Use blues, greens and greys.

Movement and Drama:

1. Look at the movement of the waves. Using finger, hand and wrist movements, finally the whole body, make slow wave movements across the hall. Make up sea music on percussion instruments.
2. Look at the movement of gulls. Move, riding the air with ease, then swoop down as a fishing boat approaches. Make deep, whole body movements, bending low at the knees.
3. Look for movement words describing water/waves/boats. (See Language Activities.) Using this list, work in twos, one miming a particular movement word, the other guessing. Read all the poems again to add to your list.
4. Imagine that you have found your own island. (See Creative Activities.) Search the island from end to end. Remember to keep a look-out for animals, snakes and large creeping things which might give chase. Bend low to go under bushes, reach up to get coconuts, bananas or other things good to eat; climb trees to see where you are.

WATER

Rivers, Lakes and Ponds

All-weather friend

Three ducks swim across the pond,
pinpricked by springtime rain;
David, in wellies,
throws bread from a bag,
says it's his favourite game.

Three ducks sail across the water,
flat-ironed by a summer sun;
David, in shorts,
scatters crumbs all around.
Lots of children join in the fun.

Three ducks battle against the waves,
feather-veined by an autumn chill;
David, in anorak,
flings crusts on the ground,
knowing that no-one else will.

Three ducks slither over the ice,
polished bright to winter's gloss;
David, fur-booted,
shares cake with all three
to honour the spirit of Christmas.

Moira Andrew

The river

Some days
the river slips
so quietly under the bridge,
you can hardly tell
it's moving.

Other days
the river rushes
so quickly under the bridge,
you wonder
what all the hurry is about.

John Foster

The Creek

Metallic jink of rigging in the wind
A shingle shore
The smell of mud and ooze
A torn sky patched by clouds
The squealing cries
of hungry gulls
The waking boats
that bob and rise
as the creek fills.

Sue Cowling

The pond

Today
the pond is still
and smooth as a mirror.
One duck is floating,
colourful as a circus clown.

Look there,
deep in the pond
there are clouds, the sky,
and one daft duck
floating upside down.

Wes Magee

The waterfall

Over rugged rocks
the water
fall
tumbles

In winter
it gasps and shouts
and
grumbles

In summer
it goes quiet, just whispers
and
mumbles

Wes Magee

When I went fishing

With a jam jar
on a length of string
I went fishing in the stream.
A long, hot day went by.

I took my catch home –
minnows and a stickleback.
All day the sun stood still
shining in the wide, wide sky.

Wes Magee

River recipe

Take 10 drops of water
from a tap
Add a pinch of salt
from a cellar
Multiply it by one
million million million
And what have you got?
A river!

Sue Stewart

Rivers, Lakes and Ponds

Visits: The children may be able to visit a local pond, watch the fishermen, feed the ducks. If a river visit is possible, it would be useful to contrast the small beginnings of rivers such as the Severn and the Thames with the 'busy-ness' and width as they near the sea. Town children can visit boating lakes in the parks, walk the Docks Trail, go to see the local reservoir. Many schools have conservation ponds and the children can be encouraged to note changes across the seasons.

Discussion and Observation:

- Look at the movement of water on the surface of the river, lake, pond. Does the weather make a difference? (See Moira Andrew's poem 'All-weather friend' and John Foster's 'The river').
- Look at the movement of gulls, ducks, frogs, tadpoles etc.
- Look at the reflections of trees, bridges, sky. (See Wes Magee's poem, 'The pond').
- Look at the ripples which boats, swans, ducks, moorhens leave behind them.
- Throw a pebble into the water and watch the ripples.
- Look at the way a waterfall or a fountain splashes and falls. Look at the pattern the water makes. (Read Wes Magee's 'The waterfall'.)
- Listen to the sound of a waterfall, a fountain. Listen to the sound of a stream or a river as it flows along.
- Look at what happens when the river or the stream has to pass over rocks.
- Look for the homes of those animals and birds who live on the river, lake, pond.
- Stand on a bridge and watch what happens to a twig or a dry leaf. Which way is the river flowing? How can you tell?
- Feed the ducks. Watch how they swim towards you, how they push one another aside to get to the bread.
- Trail your hand in the water. Feel whether the water is cold or warm.
- Watch how different water birds look when the lake or pond is covered in ice. Watch people skating.
- Listen to the sound of boats' rigging jingling in the wind. (Read Sue Cowling's poem 'The creek').

Classroom Activities:

1. Keep a diary for the conservation pond throughout the year. Note all the changes in the plants, the animals, insects and birds who live in or around the pond. This might be a class or group activity. Cut the finished diary into the shape of the pond. Put drawings, notes and photographs into it.
2. Do some pond-dipping. Take a jar to the pond and dip it into the water. Use a magnifying glass to see what weed or insects you have caught. With the help of reference books, try to identify everything. Make wall-charts of the results.
3. Experiment with bridge building. Let one group use construction kits. Another group can use ordinary classroom materials like rulers, string, counting blocks etc. to build with. Test your bridges with different loads. Which is the strongest? Can you think of the reason? (Read John Foster's 'The river'.)

Rivers, Lakes and Ponds

4. Read Sue Cowling's 'The Creek'. Make paper boats. Put them into an empty bowl. Gradually fill the bowl with water. Watch how they rise and float. 'The waking boats/that bob and rise/as the creek fills.'
5. Look at a local map. Follow the nearest river from source to mouth. Make a wall map, noting places of interest along the length of the river. Put in all the castles, parks, places you have visited. Mark where the school is placed in relation to the river. Put in the bridges. Make this map very individual to yourself and your own school.
6. Make an underwater mirror using a can with both ends cut out. (Watch out

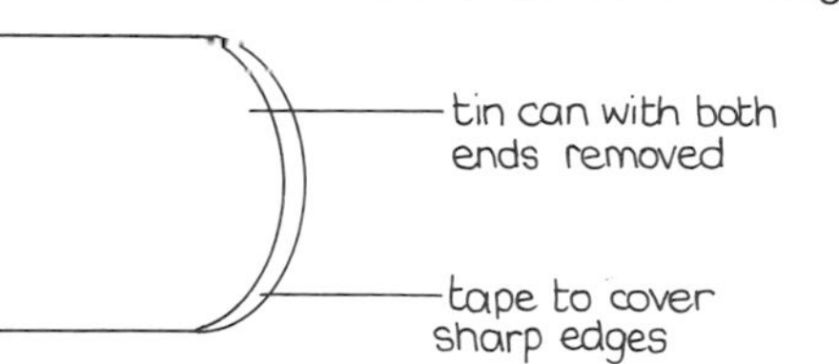

for sharp edges. Bind the edges with tape.) Fix some clear plastic over one end. Smooth out, and fix in position with elastic bands drawn tight. Put this end just under the surface of the water in the pond, and you will see some of the underwater life. Make drawings of all the creatures you see moving. Take care to get an adult's permission before you try this out.

Language Activities:

1. Read Wes Magee's poem 'The Waterfall'. Look at the way he has suggested water tumbling and splashing in a waterfall by arranging words and letters in a shape. Make shape poems which use the same ideas for 'The River', 'The Stream', 'Bridges'.
2. Read Sue Stewart's 'River recipe'. She follows the pattern of a cookery recipe very closely. Make up some recipe poems for a mountain, a rainbow, clouds, the moon. Make your recipes as unusual and imaginative as you can. You might like to look up some real recipes before you begin.
3. Look at the lake or the pond on a calm day. See how the trees, the ducks, your face looking down, the clouds are mirrored. Talk and write about the reflections. Note the way they wobble and move, the way they are broken up. See if your writing can mirror this broken image – perhaps by breaking up

Rivers, Lakes and ponds

your lines in unusual places. Read Wes Magee's poem 'The pond'. (See also Creative Activities.)

4. Read Moira Andrew's poem 'All-weather friend'. It uses the simple idea of the pond at each season of the year. The child in the poem wears different clothes to suit the weather. Make up a poem or a story about your local pond/lake/river at each season of the year. Look at the different colours, the different movement of the water, the weather.
5. Use a map to trace a local river from source to estuary. (See Classroom Activities.) Talk about the places it flows through, moorland, villages, towns, fields, woods, dockland etc. Think how different all these places will be: the sounds, what can be seen, the smells etc. Imagine that you are a twig, a fish, a water sprite, a paper boat floating/swimming the length of the river. Write a story or make up a comic book, putting in all the different scenes and places as you pass. You could make it a real river, or imagine a far-off river in a far-off land. Make it an exciting story of magic and adventure.
6. Read 'When I went fishing' by Wes Magee. The boy has spent a long happy summer's day all alone by the stream, 'A long hot day went by.' Tell about your hobby, how you like to fill your leisure time when you don't have to go to school, and can do just what you enjoy. Do you like to be alone, or would you rather be with other people? Make your report so interesting that others will say, 'That's a good idea. I'd like to do that too!'

Creative Activities:

1. Read 'The pond' by Wes Magee. In the second verse he tells how all the clouds are reflected in the pond, 'and one daft duck/floating upside down.' Make some reflection pictures by putting blobs of coloured paint on sugar paper and folding it. You will get a symmetrical pattern, looking like a reflection. You could use a selection of blues and greens to look like water. You might do a quick painting of a pond with trees, clouds etc. on one side of your paper. Fold while still wet and you will find a pond picture, with its reflections when you unfold the paper (See Language Activities.)
2. Read Wes Magee's poem 'The waterfall'. Make a group picture pasting on cut-out rocks and stones as the background to a waterfall. (Make the picture tall and narrow.) Then use torn tissue paper pasted flat and overlapping to give the effect of water tumbling down. You might add a few scraps of foil to make it look as though the water was catching the sunlight. Paint grasses and reeds to finish your picture.
3. Make several pictures of a pond or lake you have visited. Use no more than three colours, and keep the colours soft, e.g. blue, grey, white; or green, and two shades of brown. Make some of the pictures fairly small, others about A4 size. When the pictures are quite dry, cut out the bits you like best, so that you have eight or ten small rectangular pictures. Assemble the pictures collage-fashion to make a picture pattern. Leave no white spaces. You might need to overlap the pictures.

The three colours used again and again for different versions of the same view is remarkably effective, and can be made to look like a patchwork quilt.

Rivers, Lakes and Ponds

4. Read John Foster's 'The river'. Look for pictures of bridges in your reference and picture books. See how many bridge shapes you can find. Ask each person in a group to draw a different bridge using black pen, so that the structure is very clear. Copy the photographs or pictures as accurately as you can. Cut and mount the bridges each with a black mount and display them as a collection of bridge shapes, perhaps with some notes about the bridges printed beneath each example.
5. Use your pond mirror or the chart showing the results of the pond-dipping. Use felt-tip pens to draw each creature you have found. Cut these out. On a sugar paper background paint an underwater view of the pond. Use cool greens and greys on wet paper to suggest waving water weed, pebbles etc. When the background is dry, paste on your creatures and fish, so that they make an attractive pattern. You might wish to label all the creatures. Use rounded shapes to make the labels.
6. Read Sue Cowling's 'The creek'. Close your eyes and imagine all the sights and sounds. Choose the medium that you like to use best, felt-tips, wax crayons, or paint. Work in silence. Make a picture of the poem, just as you see it in your mind's eye. It should look very different from your neighbour's because a good poem will create a different picture in each person's imagination. You might like to listen to a piece of music on tape as you work.

Drama and Movement:

- Read John Foster's 'The river'. Work in groups of four or five. Let two people make a bridge. Think about the shape of your bridge – arched or suspended? Let the others move, head to toe through the bridge, first as 'the river slips', then as 'the river rushes'. Find other words and movements to describe the flow of the river and mime these. The 'bridge pair' should try to guess the movement words. Change places.

Water, Water Everywhere

Three taps

A silver tap
fills the red bowl
in the kitchen sink.

A golden tap
drips in our bathroom.
Plink. Plonk. Plink.

A rusty tap
runs by the garden wall,
gives the birds a drink.

Wes Magee

Water All Around

In a blue radox sea
three plastic ducks
turn circles
while a small white one,
wound up, flaps red legs up
and down as it moves towards
the taps.

Beneath the blue surface
a submarine shadows
the ducks.

The water is calm.
A hand lowers through water
triggers the sub's red button –
whoosh – a torpedo careers
after the little white duck,
misses and hits a big toe
by the cold tap.

Who plays this game?

John Fairfax

This morning my dad shouted

This morning my dad shouted.
This morning my dad swore.
There was water through the ceiling.
There was water on the floor.
There was water on the carpets.
There was water down the stairs.
The kitchen stools were floating
So were the dining chairs.

This morning I've been crying.
Dad made me so upset.
He shouted and he swore at me
Just 'cause things got so wet.
I only turned the tap on
To get myself a drink.
The trouble was I didn't see
The plug was in the sink.

John Foster

Water

Water has no taste at all.
Water has no smell;
Water's in the waterfall,
In pump, and tap, and well.

Water's everywhere about;
Water's in the rain,
In the bath the pond, and out
At sea it's there again.

Water comes into my eyes
And down my cheeks in tears,
When Mother cries, 'Go back and try
To wash behind those ears.'

John R. Crossland

Water's for . . .

Water's for . . . washing, drinking
making tea,
cleaning the bath
or scrubbing me;
shining a car
or rinsing a shirt
watering tomatoes,
shifting the dirt
. . . my Mum says.

But *I* say . . . paddling in wellies
or just in feet
(puddles are good
but sea's a treat)
squirting at brothers,
splashing Dad,
soaking my sister
to make her mad!
Mixing with mud
to bake a pie,
spraying the dog
or catching a fly.
Bath or puddle,
sleet or rain,
let's all play
a WATER game!

Judith Nicholls

Water, Water, everywhere

Discussion and Observation:

- Talk about our need for water; for drinking (tea, coffee, squash, juice etc.), for washing, for bathing, for cooking. (Read 'Water's for . . .' by Judith Nicholls.)
- Listen to the sounds of rain; how it changes, in a drizzle, shower, downpour, storm.
- Listen to the sound of running water at home; in the shower, sink, bath, cistern.
- Listen to the sound of waves at the seaside, to the splashing of a waterfall or a fountain, to the running of a stream.
- Look at the shape water makes spraying from a watering can, a garden hose, the kitchen tap, a teapot.
- Look at dew on the grass, leaves after rain, tears on a baby's cheeks.
- Look at the way water appears to change colour in different lights, at different depths.
- Look at a glass of water. Is it truly colourless? Sit it in the sun on a window ledge and look at it again. How has it changed?
- Talk about the need flowers, vegetables, trees and other plants have for water. Look at what happens to seedlings when they dry up.
- Talk about what happens when there is too much water, burst pipes, storms, floods. (Read John Foster's 'This morning my Dad shouted'.)
- Watch what happens when water is frozen, is boiled. (Be very careful. Steam is highly dangerous.)
- Touch and taste an ice cube.
- Look at ice forming on puddles on a winter's day. Watch how it melts in the sun.
- Look at what happens to salt and sugar in warm water.

Water, Water, everywhere

- Make soap bubbles. Look at the colours. Watch them float away.
- Taste and smell water. (Read John R. Crossland's poem 'Water'.)

Visits: It would be very useful if the children could visit the local waterworks or reservoir. Many Water Boards are willing to take children on a guided tour. This kind of visit brings home to children the importance of having clean water in plenty, and helps them appreciate our good fortune in having water available at the turn of a tap.

The children can also think about water in streams, rivers, ponds and at the seaside; the movement and sounds of water, when they make other out-of-school visits.

Classroom Activities:

1. Following out-of-school visits, note how water is used for recreation. Make a list of water sports, and of the equipment needed. Stress the need for safety. (ROSPA has a leaflet on this topic.) Talk about the need to learn to swim. Make posters about water safety and learning to swim.
2. In the company of a responsible adult, learn to make tea. Follow the directions on the packet. Write out a recipe/list of instructions which others could follow to make tea, coffee, flavoured ice lollies, jellies, lemonade.
3. Make a collection of pebbles and shells. Look carefully at the colours and shapes. Now place them in a glass jar filled with water. Look at how the colours change, the shapes are distorted. Find out why this happens.
4. Read Judith Nicholls' poem 'Water's for . . .' See how many other uses you can find for water. Put them in separate lists: the things parents use water for, the things you like to do. Try washing curtains and clothes from the play house. Hang them out to dry. Do the things dry better on a windy day or a sunny day? Or do they dry best when there is sunshine and a breeze?
5. Think of all the clothes you need to keep yourself dry. Make a classroom display of clothes that protect you from the rain.
6. Find out about countries that do not have enough rain, who don't have drinking water on tap. Oxfam, Save the Children and other charities will help. Think about what it would be like to have to walk miles under a hot sun to get water from a well. You might like to correspond with children who live in these conditions. You might be able to help raise money to provide clean running water in the villages. (Again, the usual children's charities can provide information.)
7. Read John R. Crossland's 'Water'. His poem lists a number of places where water can be found. Discuss all the sources of water that you can think of. Make a wall chart to show the list in word and picture.
8. Read Wes Magee's poem 'Three taps'. If you have visited the waterworks, work in a group to make a diagram of the water system in the house. Show where the water comes in from the mains and the pipes which take it through the house to the bathroom, WC and kitchen. Don't forget to show where the dirty water gets into the drains. You might have an outside tap too, for the garden hose or the greenhouse. When your diagram is finished, make small pictures of people using water in different parts of the house.

Water, Water, everywhere

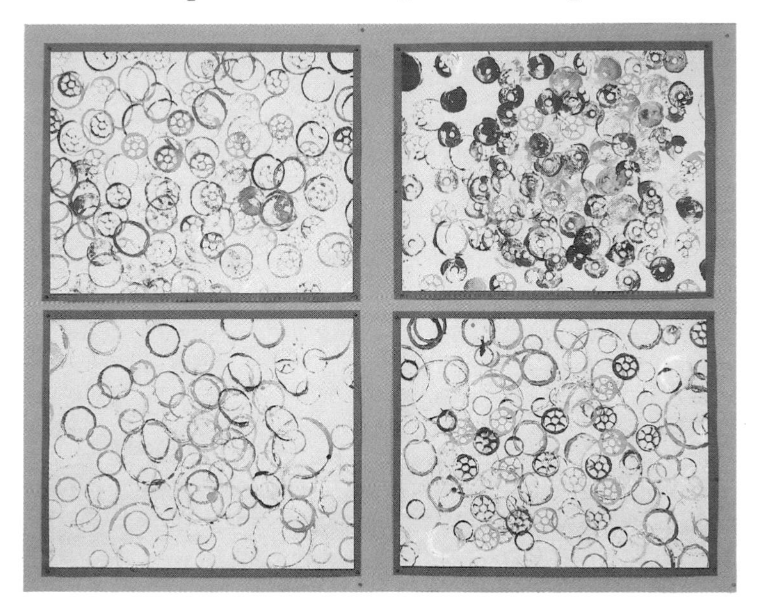

Language Activities

1. Read 'Water all around' by John Fairfax. Now write about your bath-time. Tell about the toys you play with in the bath. Tell if you like to have bath foam or if you prefer a shower with shower gel or soap-on-a-rope. Make it sound as though it is an exciting miniature world of water, e.g. 'Beneath the blue surface/a submarine shadows/the ducks.'
2. Read Wes Magee's poem 'Three taps'. Imagine that you have three different taps in your house, one gold, one silver, one bronze. But these are magic taps; nothing as boring as ordinary water comes out when you turn them on. Think about taps that pour out champagne, kiwi-fruit juice or raspberry milk-shake. Tell a story about discovering the magic taps.
3. Find as many rain words as you can. Make up a sound-song using the rain words. When you have put the words into a good rhythm, try putting music to it using percussion instruments. (Good rain music can be made from empty yogurt cartons filled with dried peas, beans and lentils. Cover with a taped-down lid made from foil or card.)
4. Read 'Water's for . . .' by Judith Nicholls. (See Classroom Activities.) Work in two groups, one suggesting all the useful things that you can do with water, the other all the things that might get children into trouble. Make up a conversation between parents and children. Use words and phrases that a fed-up dad or an annoying child would use. Make the conversation into a short play for the class to watch.
5. Make soap bubbles. (See Discussion and Observation.) Look at the colours and movements of the bubbles. Imagine that you have been given a 'Drink Me' bottle like Alice in Wonderland. You take one sip and you immediately shrink to the size of a thimble. Imagine that you have climbed into one of the bubbles and are able to go soaring away on the breeze. Tell what adventures you have, all that you see and hear. Describe how you are changed back into your own size and shape.
6. Think of the smallest drop of water in the world. Is it a dewdrop? Is it a baby's tear? Is it a drop of rain on the tip of a leaf? Write a very small poem about it. Try using no more than seventeen words. You could make your small poem into a haiku by using single-beat words, or by counting the syllables and using fewer words (five syllables in the first line, seven in the second, and five in the third).

Water, Water, everywhere

Creative Activities:

1. Make soap bubbles and watch them float into the air. (See Discussion and Observation.) Find a number of round articles for printing, e.g. corks, lids from jars (all different sizes), coins. Make a bubble pattern by printing. Dip the round shapes into fairly thick paint and press down on sugar paper. Try using just two colours, but vary the shades for the best effect. (See photograph on p. 43)
2. Read Wes Magee's 'Three taps'. Work as a group to make a three-picture panel, each picture showing a different tap, with water flowing into the kitchen sink, the bath, a bucket by the garden wall.
3. Read John Fairfax's 'Water all around'. Cut a background paper into a large oval shape, so that it looks as though you are looking down on to a bath of water. With felt-tip pens make a selection of bath toys, as colourful and as fanciful as you can. Cut these out and stick on to the bath-water background. Leave room to put the top half of a child sitting in the bath so that he/she is surrounded by toys. Find a name for your picture, e.g. 'I don't want to get out. I'm having too much fun!' (See display photograph on p. 41.)
4. Make a colour chart or a colour spiral of blues. (You might like to use a decorator's paint chart to start you off.) Begin with a bluey-white, the palest blue you can imagine. Then add a little more colour each time, going from egg-shell blue through cornflower blue to royal blue, navy blue and ultramarine. By the time you are finished, your blue should be almost black. You might like to invent words to describe every new colour you make. (John Fairfax, in his poem, talks of 'a blue radox sea'. How has he come up with this idea, do you think?)

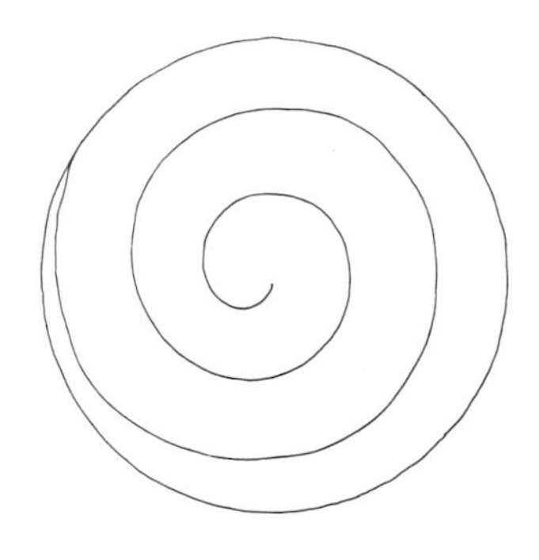

5. Read 'Water's for . . .' by Judith Nicholls. Make this poem into a group frieze with each child painting and cutting out a separate figure 'washing, drinking/making tea/cleaning the bath/or scrubbing me' and on the other side figures of children 'paddling in wellies . . . splashing Dad/soaking my sister . . .' or any other water games that you enjoy. Make this picture full of life and movement. Paint a huge hot yellow sun in the sky, and make the picture look very sunny.
6. Read John Foster's 'This morning my Dad shouted'. Paint a disaster area to do with too much water. You could make it into a comic strip, putting the story beneath the pictures, and giving the characters words to say in balloon form.

Drama and Movement:

1. Read John Foster's poem 'This morning my Dad shouted'. (See Creative Activities.) Make up dialogue to go with the poem. You might invent other disasters as well! Other characters might join the child and his/her Dad. What about Mum, sisters, brothers, the family cat? Make it realistic, but funny – funny to the audience, that is. Remember neither Dad nor the child thought it funny at the time!
2. Look at reflections in the water, then work with a partner. One person makes a shape with his/her body and the other person reflects or mirrors it. Now make it more difficult by working in fours, so that two people reflect the shape/movement of another pair. Change places.

Sunshine

My shadow

On sunny days
My shadow
Strides ahead of me
Down the street
Or stretches itself out
Behind me
Sticking to my feet.

No matter how hard I try
To shake it off
By going indoors
Or resting in the shade,
It's always there waiting for me
When I come out again.
I've tried to give it the slip
By diving in the swimming-pool,
But when I get out
It's still there,
Standing behind me
Towelling itself dry.

John Foster

The hardest thing in the world to do

The hardest thing in the world to do
is to stand in the hot sun
at the end of a long queue for ice-creams
watching all the people who've just bought theirs
coming away from the queue
giving their ice-creams their very first lick.

Michael Rosen

Sun

Sun, why do you keep staring at me,
you rude thing.

Just because you got up before me
d'you have to swank?

Bet I'm in bed first tonight.

Geoffrey Holloway

Lammas Loaf

sun conditions
the ripening grain
oven trays are big again
with loaf
and there's a sweet smell of baking bread
like fulfilment in the air –
the wheatfields
rest in peace.

Michael Henry

Sunshine

Try and hold the sunshine
in your hand –
It will slip through your fingers.

Try and catch the sunshine
as you run –
It will slide behind the hill.

But watch,
and you'll find the sunshine –
Hidden in a flower,
Beaming in a smile,
And sparkling like a secret
In your best friend's eyes.

Dave Ward

Summer sun

Yes,
the sun shines
bright
in the summer,
and the breeze
is soft
as a sigh.

Yes,
the days are
long
in the summer,
and the sun
is king
of the sky.

Wes Magee

Cat-nap

Cats can have too much
of the sun.
They sink
like stones into deep wells
of shade
beneath bushes,

their eyes shining
black
as wet pebbles.

They lie submerged until
the cool
of night.

Moira Andrew

Sunshine

Discussion and Observation:

No problems attached to getting children out into the sunshine! Encourage them to explore everything around them with heightened senses.

- Look at the colours of flowers, leaves, sky.
- Look at the way people dress for hot sunshine.
- Look at the way your shadow follows you across the playground/playing field/road. (See John Foster's poem, 'My shadow'.)
- Hold up your hand against the sun. Look at the way you can almost see your bones shining through the skin. Try to catch a handful of sunshine. (See Dave Ward's poem.) What happens?
- Look at the way cats and dogs hide from the sun. (See Moira Andrew's poem.) What about people? What happens to us if we stay out too long in the sun?
- Look at the way flowers droop in the heat of the sun. How do they look in the morning before the sun gets high into the sky?
- Look at daisies. See how they close up at night, and open their petals again in the morning.
- Watch out for butterflies, bees and other insects. Look at their colours and movements.
- Listen to the sounds of children playing outside in the sun.
- Listen to the sounds of insects.
- Listen to the sound of the ice-cream van. (See Michael Rosen's poem.)
- Feel the heat of the sun on your skin. Touch hot sand, rocks, walls, the outsides of buildings. Feel how they hold the heat.
- Taste how good ice-cream/cold drinks/ice lollies are on a hot day. Why do we enjoy them so much?
- Smell summer flowers. Which scents do you like best? Are there any flowers that do not have a perfume?

Classroom Activities:

1. Read John Foster's 'My Shadow'. Make shadow monsters with your fingers against a sunny wall. On a sunny morning go outside in pairs and mark the length of your shadow, first thing. Measure it again at break time, lunchtime, home time, and see what happens. Make a shadow graph.
2. Choose a sunny morning and set a stick into the ground.

   Note the time, and mark the position of the shadow made by the stick. Chart the shadow at each hour of the school day and find out what kind of pattern the shadows have made. You might be able to make a sundial using this idea.

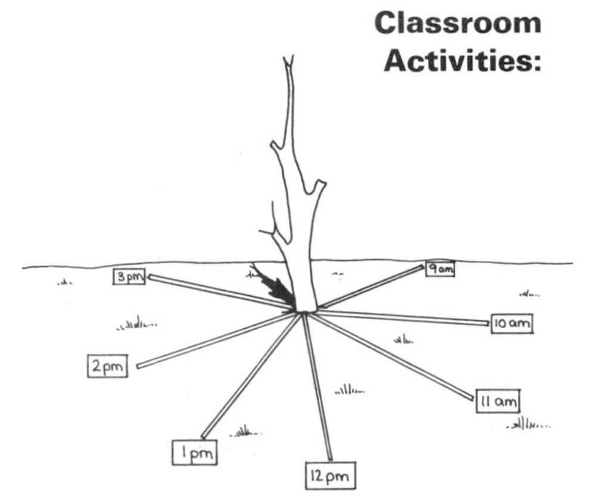

3. Read Wes Magee's poem 'Summer Sun'. Find out when the sun is highest in the sky. Find out about the longest day and the shortest day. Work out how many hours of daylight there are today, and make a pie chart (marked out in 24 sections) showing the hours of daylight in yellow, the hours of darkness in black or dark blue. Do the same thing again on the same date next month, and note the change.
4. Read Michael Henry's poem, 'Lammas loaf'. Find out at what time of the year Lammas is celebrated, and why Michael Henry writes that 'oven trays are big again/with loaf'. See if you can track down any other festival days which are connected with sunshine or fire.

Sunshine

5. Read 'Lammas Loaf' again. Find a recipe for bread. You might be able to bake bread in school – parents may offer to help. Smell the bread baking and taste how good new bread is, warm from the oven. How many different kinds of loaf do you know about? Collect recipes and pictures of bread and set up a display in the classroom. You might be able to visit a local baker's to see (and smell) bread in the making.

6. Look at animals on a hot sunny day. Watch how they move. How do they keep cool? Have you seen dogs or horses on the seashore on hot days? Where do cows and sheep and horses in the fields find shelter from the sun? Read Moira Andrew's poem 'Cat-nap'.

7. Look for all the insects you can find enjoying the sunshine. Try to identify them.

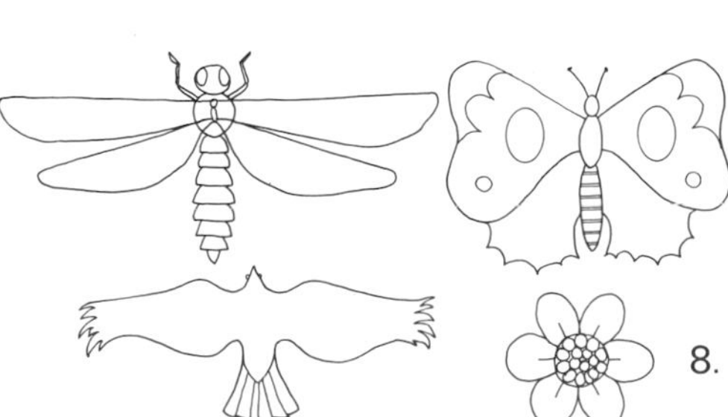

   Look for butterflies. Copy their markings and make blot patterns using bright paint. (See front cover.) How many other symmetrical shapes can you find? Make a symmetry display under a bright golden sun.

8. Read Michael Rosen's poem. Discuss what each child thinks would be the hardest thing to do. Think about waiting for a party to begin, seeing all the good things and not being allowed to touch them. Think about Christmas morning and waiting to open presents. Think about the night before your birthday.

Language Activities:

1. Read Wes Magee's poem 'Summer Sun'. He says that 'the sun/is king/of the sky'. Think about the moon. Perhaps the moon could be called 'queen of the sky'. Look at the pattern Wes Magee has used for his poem and write a similar poem about the moon.

Sunshine

2. Read Michael Rosen's poem. (See Classroom Activities, No. 8.) Now use some of the ideas you have thought about, and write your own poem called 'The hardest thing in the world to do'. Don't make it too long.
3. If you have baked bread after reading Michael Henry's 'Lammas loaf' (See Classroom Activities, No. 5), work as a group and collect together all the recipes you have found. Each person should choose a different recipe and write it out, watching that each step in the process is easy to follow. Illustrate the recipes in black and white, using a fine felt-tip pen. Put all the recipes together to make a book about making bread. If you have the pages photocopied, you might be able to sell copies to raise money towards your favourite charity.
4. Read Geoffrey Holloway's short poem called simply 'Sun'. He is thinking of the sun as a huge staring eye. Try to use some other image for the sun, e.g. a beach ball/a pound coin/a yellow lollipop, and try to use that idea in a short poem with a question. Samantha wrote this copy-cat poem.

   'Sun, why have you floated so high,
   into the sky?
   Just out of my reach, no matter how
   I stretch I can't catch your string.

   Bet you burst on the church tower,
   (Serve you right!)'

   What image has Samantha used for the sun?
5. Here is a memory game. Sit in a circle. The first person says, 'I'm going on holiday to the sun. I've packed my suitcase and I've taken my sun hat. . .' The next person has to remember what went before and must add her own suggestion for something suitable to take on a sunshine holiday. The first person to make a mistake is out. You could develop this game into a list poem, ending it with 'But I forgot my bathing costume/sun oil/toothbrush/airline ticket'.
6. Read John Foster's poem 'My shadow' and Moira Andrew's 'Cat-nap'. Think about how lovely it is to find a cool spot on a hot day. Think about where these dark shadowy places are. Write a poem using all the cool grey words you can think of. Imagine that you have found this welcome place well away from the sun and the sounds of other children playing, where you can be quite alone. Imagine yourself sinking 'like a stone into deep wells/of shade/beneath bushes' (or wherever) looking out into a world yellow with sunshine.

Creative Activities:

1. Read Michael Rosen's poem. Work as a group, each painting a single child dressed for a hot day in brightly patterned shorts/dress/bathing costume. When the paintings are dry, cut out the figures. Paint an ice-cream van and one child going away with a large ice-cream cornet. Paste all the other figures in a long queue waiting, waiting for their turn to come at the ice-cream van. Don't forget to paint in a bright golden sun. (See display photograph on p. 47.)
2. Read Michael Henry's 'Lammas loaf'. Look for all the different loaf shapes you can find. (See Classroom/Language Activities.) Work as a group, each painting a large loaf. (Look carefully at the bread and paint in the shadows and curves of the bread and crust.) Then cut the loaves out and pile on to a big painted tray – 'oven' trays are big again/with loaf'. Pile the loaves one on top of the other so that the picture looks very full.

Sunshine

3. Take a bowl of water into the sun, and make ripples with your hands or drop a stone into the water. Look at the patterns on the surface. Make a pattern picture using wax crayons or oil-based pastels. Leave out the figures and concentrate on the pattern of sun on water.
4. Bring in a bunch of dandelions or marigolds. Paint a picture of lots of marigolds/dandelions/sunflowers growing. Make them as bright as you can. Now paint the sun in the corner of the picture and see if you can make it outshine the flowers.
5. Read 'Sun' by Geoffrey Holloway. Make a picture of a child in bed, showing the window of the room. Make a big bright sun outside the window because it is mid-summer and he/she has had to go to bed in daylight.
6. Read 'Summer Sun' by Wes Magee. Make a picture of the sun as a king in a shining crown. Use cut foil paper to make the crown and try to make it as rich looking as possible. You might have a lot of little people standing on earth looking up at King Sunshine in the sky. What kind of clothes would they be wearing, do you think?
7. Look at the long dark shadows made by the setting sun. Read John Foster's poem 'My shadow'. Now paint a group of people standing on a hill watching the sunset, and give each person his/her own long dark shadow. Watch the kind of reflected group pattern the shadows make. Keep most of your colour in the bright yellow/orange/red setting sun and the long dark shadows.

Drama and Movement:

1. Read Michael Rosen's poem. (See Language and Creative Activities.) Let one child be the ice-cream man. Let the others wait in the queue. Show by the way you stand and in your expression that waiting 'in the hot sun/at the end of a queue for ice-creams' is the hardest thing in the world to do.
2. Read John Foster's 'My Shadow'. Work with a partner. Let one person 'stride down the street' or 'stretch out'. As he/she moves, the partner must stick very closely, following and repeating each movement like a shadow. Try to give your shadow the slip 'By diving in the swimming pool' but the shadow is 'always there waiting for me'. Try to outwit your shadow. Then change places.

Rain

shower

fierce
spring
rain
full
gushing
drain
grey
puddled
street
Wellies
for
feet
drab
steely
sky
umbrellas
held
high
children
want
out
harassed
mothers
shout
cars
make
spray
birds
huddle
away
cats
lie
asleep
plants
drink
deep
rain
becomes
drops
slows
and
stops
doors
open
wide
people
step
outside.

Moira Andrew

Grumpy and Gruff (song)

There was an old couple called Grumpy and Gruff,
They lived in the weather which was windy enough.
They had an umbrella to keep the rain off,
And one had a sneeze and the other a cough.

Now someone felt sorry for Gruffy and Grump
So he bought them a palace – though some say a dump.
And the stars all fell silent with the housewarming din.
There was *weather* without, but the two were within.

Gerda Mayer

Flood

The rain fell all night, beating on roofs
as dark and hunched as hills,
cascading uncontained into the street
in wind-curved waterfalls.

All night the rain fell, kept falling.
This morning, the street's a river:
cars founder and sink, while buses
crawl laden as ocean liners,

raise bow-waves so swollen they break
booming across the pavement
where tossed at the tide's rising mark
seaweed tangles to litter.

And under the hedges and gates
fish shoal in the gleaming shallows,
and further out, through the channel
marked by wave-slapped traffic lights,

dolphins leap lampposts, and whales
surge and sound in the deep roads.

Dave Calder

a puddle-skrinkling day

it's a crinkly, crankly
chill kind of day

if I tip-toe on the
puddles they splinter away

tip toe crispy-crunchy
up and down the lane

skrinkle all the puddles
then tip-toe home again.

Joan Poulson

Rain

Listen . . .
the trees are breathing
under the rain.
They have waited for weeks,
and this is their special
minute.
You can watch the trembling dancers
tiny as grain –
the line drops softly quivering
as they jump –
a touch will begin it.

It's a day for boots,
for the big buds of umbrellas
opening everywhere
like sudden flowers.
It's a day for splashing in gutters.
Down the lane
surely there's no roof
half so drenched as ours?
Listen . . .
the trees are brooding
under the rain.

Jean Kenward

Rain

Discussion and Observation: On a wet day let the children go outside (clad for the weather!) to find out as much as they can about rain, using their senses. The class could be divided into groups: listening, looking, feeling – even smelling and tasting.

- Listen to the sound of rain on leaves, the grass, the tops of cars, the roof. Does it always sound the same? Find words to describe the sounds, or make up nonsense words to sound like different kinds of rainy weather.
- Listen to the sound of raindrops on an umbrella, an anorak hood, a sou'wester.
- Listen to the different rhythms rain makes in a drizzle, a shower, a downpour. Listen to the slow way rain drips from leaves and branches after a shower is over.
- Look at the way rain flows down gutters and gratings, the way it hangs in drops on the tips of leaves, the way it makes the grass shine. Look at the patterns it makes in puddles. Look at the way a cat walks in the wet, the way a bird shakes its feathers.
- Look at the patterns rain makes on windows, the car windscreen, on the surface of a pond.
- Smell the earth after rain, damp coats hanging in the cloakroom, wet pavements after a sudden shower.
- Turn your face up to the rain. Feel it on your cheeks. Let raindrops drip off your nose, between your fingers. Tell how your feet feel in damp shoes.
- Taste rain on your tongue.
- Wearing wellies, walk or jump in puddles. Sail stick or leaf boats in puddles in the playground.

Rain

Classroom Activities:

1. Listen to the sound of rain, to the rhythms it makes. (See Discussion and Observation.) Make up rain music using percussion instruments, and add to it your own rainy day words, either from a word list, or nonsense words which reflect the sounds of rain. (See Joan Poulson's poem, 'a puddle-skrinkling day'.)
2. Plant two lots of seeds. Put one tub outside in the rain, leave the other indoors without water. Watch what happens.
3. Collect samples of all the kinds of clothing that we wear to keep out the wet. Talk about the protection that coats, boots, anoraks and umbrellas give us, and sort them into sets. Find different ways to make up your sets, e.g. materials, which parts of the body are protected, whether the clothes are suitable for a damp day, a showery day, a very wet day etc.
4. Look for newspaper reports about flooding. (See Dave Calder's poem 'Flood'.) Talk about what you would save first if your house was threatened with flooding. Talk about the way you might escape from the water. Talk about how different your street might look in a flood – only the upstairs windows visible, using the bedroom window as a door, sitting on the roof, boats instead of cars going along the street. Then imagine what it might be like if fish came swimming up the road and into your house.

   'dolphins leap lampposts, and whales
   surge and sound in the deep roads.'
5. Make and keep a weather chart. Mark it out in squares and glue a cut-out symbol on for each day. See how many different symbols you can find for rain. (The weather forecasters usually use clouds, but there are many more interesting ways of showing wet days.) Count in the weekends and find out which is the rainiest month.
6. Read 'Grumpy and Gruff' by Gerda Mayer.

   Find out how many ways there are of forecasting the weather: weathercock, rhymes (e.g. 'A red sky at night/ Shepherds' delight/Red sky in the morning/Shepherd's warning'), barometer, weather house with husband and wife like Grumpy and Gruff.

   Make your own weather house so that you can show rain or shine.
7. Make some little boats from dry leaves/sticks/paper or other scraps. Try them out in the water tank in the classroom to find out which will float best. Then take them outside after rain and race them across the puddles. You might be able to play a game of 'Pooh-sticks' with a friend.
8. Look at the way people hurry to get out of the rain. Think about those who have to work in all weathers, heavy rain included: shepherds, policemen, fishermen etc.

Language Activities:

1. Read newspaper cuttings about flooding. (See Classroom Activities.) Read 'Flood' by Dave Calder. Imagine that you are a newspaper reporter coming along to find out how people feel about the event. Ask different people in the class to tell their stories about what has happened to them. You will need to think up some interesting questions. Note down what has been said, then write up your report in columns like a newspaper. You might like to illustrate some of these, as there are sure to be photographers at the scene.

Rain

2. Make a list of all the rain words you can find, and print them on a rainy day wall chart in the shape of a huge umbrella. Read 'shower' by Moira Andrew, and see if you can make a similar list poem using some of the words from the wall card. Remember to slant the words across the paper so that they make a shape poem.
3. Read 'a puddle-skrinkling day' by Jean Poulson. Think of the rhythms of rain and make up some new rain words to go with them, e.g. 'skrinkle all the puddles'. You might like to put those words to music (see Classroom Activities No. 1) and make up your own rain song.
4. Think of what it would be like if there were no rain. What would happen to the grass and flowers? How would you make tea and coffee? How would you get washed? In very dry countries the people sometimes make up rain songs and dances to encourage the 'rain gods' to send some rain, so that the crops will not die and everyone will have enough to eat. Make up a rain song and dance using your new rain words and the rhythms of rain on percussion instruments. Make the song sound very magic and mysterious.
5. Tell or write about getting ready to go to the beach/an outing to the park/the school fair. The weather forecast has promised hot sunshine, so you set off in high spirits. Tell what happens when you are caught in a downpour, dressed for the sun.
6. Look at the way cows stand huddled together on a wet day, the way hens shake their feathers, the neat way a cat picks its way through the puddles, shaking each paw as it goes. Imagine that you are a creature who doesn't like wet days. Begin a poem with 'I hate the rain . . .' then tell how you hide, shake yourself, walk in the rain etc., but do not tell who or what you are. Give lots of clues in the poem, and end it with a question, 'What am I?' This kind of guessing poem is called a riddle.
7. Listen to the sounds of rain. (See Discussion and Observation.) Then read Jean Kenward's poem, 'Rain'. She begins and ends her poem with the word 'Listen . . .' standing by itself on one line. Make a list of all the sounds you have heard, e.g. rain dripping from the roof, the swish of windscreen wipers, children splashing through puddles, and make up a rain poem beginning 'Listen'. Just list on separate lines the things you have heard. Read them over so that they sound good. Lists are a very good way of writing interesting poems.

Creative Activities:

1. Paint the head and shoulders of a child, perhaps looking rather sad. She wants to go outside to play, but it is too wet. Put her behind a window and make rain with cellophane or cut straws. Make the rain very heavy so that it looks like a real downpour.

Rain

2. Read Dave Calder's 'Flood', and newspaper accounts of flooding. Work as a group and make a frieze of a street with houses, shops, a school, a church and a pub. All these buildings could be painted separately, cut out and pasted on the background. When everything is dry, make a flooded street from cut paper and tissue paper. Use shades of blue and green, with some white. Then put boats filled with people on the water, people waiting to be rescued at upstairs windows, on the roof, up trees. When you get to the end of the poem 'Flood' you will find that the streets have dolphins and whales swimming along them. You could add some bright silver and gold fish made from foil.
3. Read Jean Kenward's poem 'Rain'. She says

   'It's a day for boots,
   for the big buds of umbrellas
   opening everywhere
   like sudden flowers.'

   Each person in a group should paint a child dressed for the rain. Make their clothes look rather grey and drab. Cut out the figure when it is dry. Paste on to a blue background, placing them in a group. Now paint bright umbrellas, one for each figure, making them look like 'sudden flowers'. Again it is best to paint, cut out and paste. You might like to add foil or cellophane raindrops, and put puddles at their feet. (See display photo, p. 51.)
4. Read 'a puddle-skrinkling day' by Jean Poulson. Look at the patterns rain makes on the surface of puddles. Use white wax crayons or candles to make a rain pattern, then wash over with thin paint. This will make a wax resist rain pattern. Mount several together on the wall to make a rainy day display. A selection of rain words could be printed underneath.
5. Make a group picture of a rain forest. Use wet paper for the background, and paint in lots of trees close together. Make it look very jungly with creepers and leafy plants. When it is dry, paste on all the creatures who live in the rain forest. Make them very bright, using felt-tip pens. Don't forget the birds who live there too.
6. Read 'Grumpy and Gruff' by Jean Kenward. Paint a weather house, with Grumpy and Gruff, one on either side. Give them bright clothes and make patterns on her skirt and his braces, using felt-tip pens. (See Classroom Activities, No. 6.)
7. Using thick wax crayons, make bright stripes across the page. Use rainbow colours. Now cover the bright colours with black wax crayon. Don't lean so heavily this time. Rest your picture on a board and scratch off a pattern of falling rain or big raindrops, using a sharp instrument. (You will need to ask your teacher what to use.) This will make a scratch picture of a dark wet day with a rainbow showing through the rain.

Drama and Movement:

1. Look at flowers in a heatwave. Look at the way they droop their heads. When the rain comes along, they slowly reach up towards it, standing tall and straight. Make your body into a drooping flower thirsting for the rain. As the rain falls, stretch up slowly, using fingers and hands, until you are straight and tall again. Don't forget that your roots will search for rain underground, so make your feet and toes stretch too.
2. Look at how different creatures move in the wet. Choose to move or hide as a creature caught in the rain. Let the others guess which creature you are. (See Language Activities, No. 6.)

Wind and Storms

wind's a funny old thing

spring it strokes your face
as if it were a baby's

summer it cools you down
when you're red with sun

autumn it gets bad tempered
throws leaves about

winter it tries to trip you up
like a bully-boy in the playground

Geoffrey Holloway

When the Wind Blows

When the wind blows
Do what you can.
Try to walk,
Try to stand.
Catch your hat
Before it flies.
Watch the clouds rattle
Across the skies.
Do what you can
When the wind blows –
But go where it takes you,
You cannot choose!

Dave Ward

The Storm

The sky is full of dragon light.
The forks of lightning flash.
The sky is full of dragon roars.
The rolls of thunder crash.

The dark clouds race across the sky.
Down comes the pouring rain.
The green shoots burst out of the earth.
The farmer smiles again.

John Foster

Predator

The wind is a wolf,
grey sleet dripping
from its fangs. It
tears wild-eyed at
trees, spitting out
branches like gnawed
chicken bones.

Moira Andrew

What's the time, Mr Dandelion?

Time to spread yellow suns
over the fields,

Time to blow minute-stars
into the sky;

Time to lie counting
lions'-teeth hours,

Time to stand still now,
watching time fly.

Judith Nicholls

It's Only the Storm

'What's that creature that rattles the roof?'
'Hush, it's only the storm.'

'What's blowing the tiles and the branches off?'
'Hush, it's only the storm.'

'What's riding the sky like a wild white horse,
Flashing its teeth and stamping its hooves?'

'Hush, my dear, it's only the storm,
Racing the darkness till it catches the dawn.
Hush, my dear, it's only the storm,
When you wake in the morning, it will be gone.'

Dave Ward

When the wind blows

When the wind blows
Coats flap, scarves flutter.

When the wind blows
Branches groan, leaves mutter.

When the wind blows
Curtains swish, papers scatter.

When the wind blows
Gates creak, dustbins clatter.

When the wind blows
Doors slam, windows rattle.

When the wind blows
Inside is a haven
Outside is a battle.

John Foster

On a Windy Day

Paper bag ghosts
On nowhere feet
Walk this way, that
Along the street.

Irene Rawnsley

Wind and Storms

Discussion and Observation:

On a windy day the children can dress up warmly and go out into the playground. Storms are best experienced from the warmth and safety of the classroom, although children will have had some experience of this kind of weather simply by going to and from school.

- Look at the effect the wind has on trees, branches and leaves.
- Look at the effect the wind has on people going about their business. Look at the way they walk against a high wind. If you are near the sea, look at the effect of wind on waves.
- Watch one particular tree, and see the effect of different kinds of windy weather, from a gentle breeze through to a full-blown storm.
- Watch for the weather forecast on television and in the newspapers.
- Talk about the idea that, although we can hear the wind, and see its effect on many things, we cannot see the wind itself.
- Listen to a gentle breeze in the trees, in the grass.
- Listen to the wind rising on a stormy day.
- Watch how birds' nests sway on the branches of trees in a high wind.
- Watch how flowers bend in the wind.
- Watch how leaves are blown across the grass in the autumn.
- Look out for seeds that are carried by the wind (See Judith Nicholls' 'What's the time, Mr. Dandelion?')
- Feel the touch of wind on your skin, stroking your face 'as if it were a baby's' in spring, tripping you up 'like a bully-boy' in winter ('wind's a funny old thing', by Geoffrey Holloway).
- Try to walk against the wind and feel how you lean into it, going where it takes you. 'You cannot choose!' says Dave Ward, in 'When the wind blows'.
- Look at the way paper and other litter is blown about in the wind. (See Irene Rawnsley's 'On a windy day'.)
- Look at how lightning lights up the sky, and listen to the thunder roll when there is a thunder and lightning storm. (See John Foster's 'The Storm'.)
- Look for the rainbow when the storm is over.
- Look at clothes flapping as they dry on the line.
- Listen to the sound of wind in the telephone wires, to bin lids rolling, to doors banging in the wind. (See John Foster's poem 'When the wind blows'.)

Classroom Activities:

1. Find out how to make a kite. Try either the traditional shape or a box kite. Use light balsa wood for the frame, and tissue paper for the covering. Make a bright tail of string with coloured paper knots tied along its length. Take the kites outside on a windy day to see how they fly.
2. Look at a dandelion head. Blow the seeds away and see how the wind disperses them. (See Judith Nicholls' poem.)

Make a miniature book, about eight pages long, to tell the story of a dandelion seed. Begin with the bright yellow head, go on to the white dandelion clock, full of seeds, then pick out just one seed and tell its story as it is taken away on the wind to grow into another flower. Illustrate each stage of the process as you tell the story. This idea could be used for other seeds which are dispersed by wind. Make a series of these little books for the classroom library.

Wind and Storms

3. Read Irene Rawnsley's poem 'On a windy day'. She writes about 'paper bag ghosts/On nowhere feet' blowing along the street. Look at the litter that collects against the playground fence after a storm. Wear plastic gloves and collect the litter in a plastic bag. Examine what kind of litter has been found. Make a display of the litter and try to think of ways to prevent such a mess. Make some anti-litter posters and display them in the school hall.
4. Collect autumn leaves that have blown down from the trees. Try to identify them. Make rubbings of the leaves using wax crayons or soft pencils, and make a frieze of the leaf shapes which you have collected. (See Geoffrey Holloway's poem. He says that the wind gets bad tempered in autumn, and 'throws leaves about'.)
5. Find out about the Beaufort Scale which measures different strengths of the wind, from a gentle breeze to a hurricane. Copy the scale on a chart and see if you can tell what kind of wind is blowing just by looking at the trees in the playground or in the street. Think of other kinds of wind which you would like to name, and make another wind-scale called by the name of your class.

Language Activities:

1. Read John Foster's poem 'When the wind blows'. You will see that every verse begins with the same line. Make up a copy-cat poem for a different kind of weather, following the pattern of John Foster's poem. Try 'When the snow falls' or 'When the sun shines', or 'When the fog drifts'. Watch the ending which has to round off the poem in some kind of way. This poem ends by contrasting inside with outside.
2. Read 'Predator' by Moira Andrew. In this poem she thinks of the wind as a wolf. Are there other animals that the wind could be compared to? Think of the wind as a cat, a hungry tiger, a mischievous puppy. Begin your poem with 'The wind is a . . .' and think of how that animal might move or look as it blows trees down, takes slates off the roof, tosses leaves.

Wind and Storms

3. Nobody has ever seen the wind. We can feel it on our faces, see its effect on the things around us, listen to the sound it makes in the night. (See Discussion and Observation.) Think this time of how the wind might look and behave if it were a person. What kind of person might do what the wind does? Susan had a good idea. She began a poem called 'What is the wind?' with the lines,

   'The wind is a wizard
   enchanting the trees.'

   Work on this poem as a group. Each person should write two lines saying who the wind is, and what he/she might do. Put these lines together to make a group poem. Write it out on a huge cut-out leaf shape or on a kite shape to display on the classroom wall.
4. Go outside on a windy day. Look and listen. Try to walk against the wind. See what happens when you take a balloon on a string or a stick with paper streamers tied to it. Feel the wind in your hair, against your face, tugging at your clothes. (See Discussion and Observation.) Go inside and write down all you can remember of your walk into the wind. Then put your ideas together in the form of a poem. Read Dave Ward's poem 'When the Wind blows'.
5. Read Irene Rawnsley's poem 'On a windy day'. She has looked very carefully at a paper bag blowing along the street. Although the poem is only four lines long, it makes a complete picture in your mind. This kind of short poem is sometimes called a snapshot because it captures a moment of time in the same way as a photograph. Look very carefully at one thing disturbed by the wind; a leaf, a crisp packet, a dustbin lid, someone's hat. Make a four or five line snapshot poem about it.
6. Read Dave Ward's poem 'It's only the storm'. Who do you think are the two people taking part in this conversation? You could make a little play out of this poem if two people each took a speaking part. Work in pairs and see if you can put together a little piece (poem, playlet, story) in which two characters take part. Write down not who they are, but what they say. Let the readers or listeners work out who the characters are from what is said. You might follow Dave Ward's pattern and write something called 'It's only the wind' or you could do something quite different, as long as you make it a conversation between two people.

Creative Activities:

1. Read Geoffrey Holloway's poem, 'Wind's a funny old thing'. Divide your paper into four and take each rectangle to make pictures of spring, summer, autumn and winter. Choose one tree and show how it might look at each season of the year. Use felt-tip pens.
2. Read Moira Andrew's 'Predator'. In this poem she writes of the wind as a wolf. There are many other animals that wind could be compared to. (See Language Activities, No. 2.) When you have written your poems giving the wind the character of an animal, try making masks to go with the poems.
3. Look carefully at a line of trees blowing in the wind. Look at the way they bend in one direction. Look at the grass or bushes beneath the trees and you will see that they are also bending in the same direction. (Read Dave Ward's 'When the wind blows'.) Use pastel or oil-based crayons to make a picture of the trees blowing in the wind. Draw all your lines in the same direction (that of the wind) and the whole picture will show a sense of rhythm and give the effect of wind blowing across your picture. (See display photograph on p. 57.)

Wind and Storms

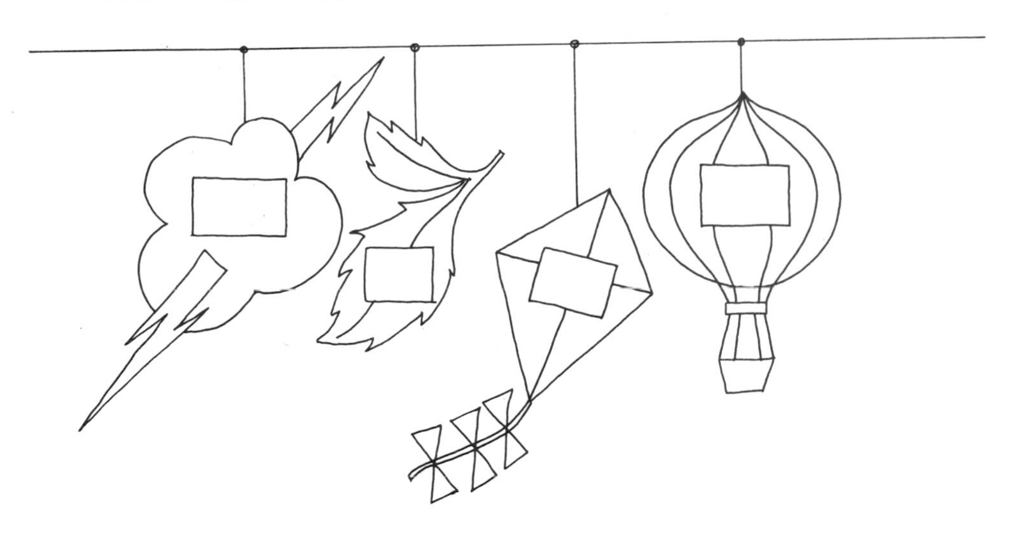

THE FLYING POETRY SHOW

4. Read John Foster's 'When the wind blows'. Make a class frieze with six groups taking part, each illustrating a verse. Try using a different medium for each picture.
5. Collect all the poems you have written about wind and storms. Write them out on both sides of large cut-out shapes of things that float or fly in the wind, e.g. leaf shapes, kites, balloons, zig-zags of lightning, and attach a string to the top. 'Fly' the poems from a string across the school hall like giant mobiles. Call your poem-mobiles 'The Flying Poetry Show'. Everyone will want to come and read them. (See line drawing above.)
6. See if you can find a book of Van Gogh's paintings. Look at the way he uses streaks of paint to give a feeling of movement to his pictures, e.g. 'Yellow Cornfield', 1889, 'Starry Night', 1889. Look closely at the effect of wind on a field of corn, on the sea, on the tops of trees, and see if you can paint a scene in the style of Van Gogh. Use your paint thick and in bold streaks of colour, painting across your picture to give the effect of the wind blowing.
7. Look at flags, streamers and pennants blowing in the wind. Choose three colours and make the pattern of each, either by painting, or by pasting down strips of tissue paper.

Drama and Movement:

1. Read Dave Ward's 'When the wind blows'. Move as though you were walking against a strong wind. 'Try to walk/Try to stand/Catch your hat/Before it flies . . .' Now work as two groups, one the wind, going from a gentle breeze to a gale, the other group responding in mime. Change places.
2. Read Dave Ward's 'It's only the storm', and expand it into a short play, making up extra words as you go along. Now try other conversations between two people, e.g. Dad, and child not wanting to go to bed; Mum, and child asking for money for ice-cream; Grandma, and child planning a treat, etc.
3. Read 'Predator' and see Creative Activities, No. 2. Wearing animal masks (with ideas from the poems) move around the hall as those animals might move. Prepare a Carnival of Wind-Animals.

Snow

On the lawn one morning

A pair of spectacles,
a hat,
a scarf,
(the knitted kind);

a stick,
a little pile of stones;
who came
and left his things behind?

Answer: A snowman

Irene Rawnsley

Overnight

Overnight,
While we slept,
The snow crept
Out of the sky
And blew its white breath
Over doorsteps and sills,
Gardens, fields and hills.
We woke to find
A world turned white
Overnight.

John Foster

Any Colour, as long as it's White

I left the garden winter-grey
when I went to bed last night.
While I slept a painter came and
emulsioned the whole place white.

The fence, the swing, my father's
car, everything whitewashed clean;
not a stain, not a mark, no dirty
footsteps anywhere to be seen.

I hurried into my wellies,
my woolly hat and my coat.
I stepped into the pure white garden
and with a stick I wrote

a poem on blank white paper
where the lawn was supposed to be.
Then I painted a picture all in white
– I had no choice, you see.

I sculpted a giant snowman,
white body, white head, white feet.
Then it started snowing again
and I had to beat a retreat.

All *my* artistic efforts were lost
under a brush that was full of snow
as the demon artist covered them up
in the one colour he seems to know!

Moira Andrew

Snow

Snow is a blanket
Silently pulled over the town at night,
Softening both sound and shapes so all in
sight
Is quietly muffled, smooth and bland,
Shapes lose their character and all the
land
Is levelled as if neatly wrapped
Like a great white parcel
And all the mapped
Landmarks are lost.

The scratchy holly's
Now a soft-skinned ball,
And mounds and shrubs and plants have all
Disappeared, while a cold lid has closed
Over the pond's bright eye.
We marvel at it. Then from the sky
The sun's slow burn
Will see the world we know
Gradually return.

John Cotton

Millionaire

Put your tongue out.
If it's long enough
you can catch all the snowflakes in the
world.

Geoffrey Holloway

Snowy Day in the Park

Across the park
the footprints go
criss-crossing crazily
over the snow . . .

Here a dog has scampered,
here a child has run,
here a mouse on tiny feet
has scuttled in the frosty grass
now sparkling in the sun.

Across the clean white page of the park
the footprints are there to be read,
and we're leaving a message for
somebody else
in the wandering patterns we tread.

Sheila Simmons

WEATHER

Snow

Discussion and Observation: There is no problem about getting the children interested in snow! At the first flake everything else is forgotten.

- Look at the way the flakes drift past the window.
- Look at the way the whiteness changes the outside world – fenceposts, goal posts, the bicycle shed – everything becomes softer and all the sharp edges are lost. Get the children into their boots and coats and take them outside to explore snow with all their senses alive.
- Listen to the quietness.
- Listen for birds, dogs, cars, children playing. Do they sound the same as usual? What might make them different?
- Put out your tongue and try to catch a snowflake. How does it taste? (Read Geoffrey Holloway's poem 'Millionaire'. Why do you think he has given it such an unusual title?)
- Look at snow lying across the playing fields/playground. Has anyone or anything crossed the snow? Look for tracks of animals and birds.
- Look at the way snow clings to roofs and branches. Look at the patterns snow makes on winter trees.
- Look at the way people dress for the snow.
- Look at the way cats and dogs move in the snow. Who do you think enjoys this weather more? A cat or a dog? Why?
- Feel the snow under your boots. Listen to the sound of your feet.
- Make a snowball and feel what happens to your hands. If you are hit by a snowball, how does it feel? What happens to boots and gloves in the snow?
- How does it feel when you go back indoors? Look at your neighbour. What happens to our faces in the snow?

Snow

- Make tracks across the playground and play 'Follow-my-leader'.
- Build a snowman. What will happen to him when the snow melts? (Read Irene Rawnsley's poem, 'On the lawn one morning'.)

Classroom Activities:

1. Find out about the different tracks which birds and animals make in the snow. Try to identify any that you have seen on the playing field/playground. (Read Sheila Simmons' poem 'Snowy day in the park' and see if you can match tracks to the creatures she writes about.)
2. Look up books to see how many snowflake patterns you can find. Have you found any that look the same? See if you can copy snowflake patterns in white paint on black paper.
3. Bring your snowy boots into the warm classroom and sit them in an empty desk tray or the caretaker's bucket. Watch what happens as the snow melts. Can you find a way of measuring how much melted snow came off your boots?
4. Make a classroom display of clothes to keep you warm in the snow. How do you keep warm at home? in bed? What kinds of food help you to keep warm? Find out about how old people manage in the cold weather.
5. Find out what birds need to keep them going in cold weather.

Make a bird table, or bird tray for the classroom window sill. Put out scraps of fat, raisins and wild bird seed. Remember to put out a saucer of water, and to replace it when ice forms on it. See how many different birds come to the bird table. Keep a daily record and see how many of them you can identify.

Language Activities:

1. Read 'Overnight' by John Foster, and 'Any Colour, as long as it's white' by Moira Andrew. Both poems tell about waking up to a white world. Tell or write about what you saw out of your window the first morning you woke up to snow. Tell what was lost under the blanket of snow, how different the familiar things looked.
2. In a group, make a list of all the things you think that snow might be like, e.g. a white bird, a pot of whitewash, feathers from a pillow. Put your list together as a set of images, leaving out the word 'like'. You might like to make the title into a question, 'What is snow?' Print the poem on white card cut into a circle to look like a snowball.
3. Design a snowman. Write out a 'recipe' for building him. Make it clear enough for someone who has never seen a snowman to be able to build it first time. First make a list of all the things you will need, (See 'on the lawn one morning'), then write out the method of building. Make a sketch of the finished snowman. (See children's work on p. 63.)
4. Describe a snowy morning in a letter to a penfriend who has never seen the snow. Tell how it feels and looks. Tell how quiet it is on a snowy morning. Make sure that you tell your friend all the wonderful games there are that make snow very special for children. Don't forget about sledging and snowball fights.

Snow

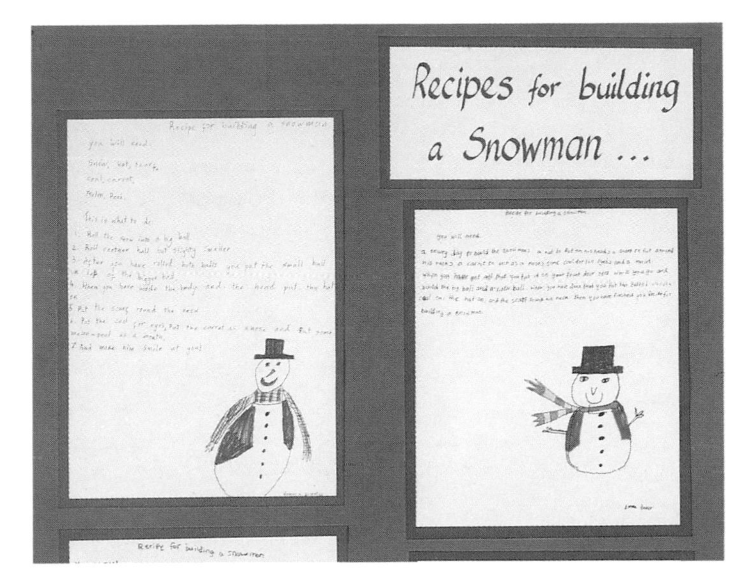

Creative Activities:

1. Read 'Snowy day in the park'. On white paper or card, make a pattern of footprints and tracks 'criss-crossing crazily/over the snow'. Use black felt-tip pen or wax crayon for the tracks and use a reference book to guide you.
2. Make a snowflake mobile for the classroom. Cut patterns out of white paper, making them as near as you can to the patterns you have found in the reference books. You might like to spray the snowflakes with glitter, then string them up from the ceiling so that they move and twirl every time the door is opened.
3. Let a group of children each paint a child dressed for the snow in boots, woolly bobble hats and flying scarves. Make some with an arm outstretched in the act of throwing, others ducking down out of the way. When the paint is dry, cut the figures out and place on a dark backing. Paste them down in two groups. Then paint in the snow underfoot and paint some large snowballs flying in the air. Make this group picture full of action, with lots of colour in hats and scarves, and large enough to be a wall panel.
4. Make a frieze of bare trees, using black or dark grey paint. Put a fence in the picture, or some spiky winter bushes. Then dip your fingers in white paint and put finger-painted snow all over your picture. This way of working makes the snowflakes less dense than straight paint. Remember to put snow on top of the fence and on the bushes. You might like to put some birds huddling in the branches, or some creatures making their way through the snow. Don't forget to put in tracks to show where they have come from. (See display photograph, p. 61.)

Snow

5. Read John Cotton's 'Snow'. In a group, make the outline of a town in black ink. (Dip a black felt-tip in a little water for a very unusual effect.) Gradually build up snow on and around the buildings, using scraps of white tissue paper pasted flat, one over the other. Don't put any snow falling in this picture, but paint in a huge bright sun in one corner of the sky. Make it yellow and orange and red, like the sun in winter.

   'Then from the sky
   The sun's slow burn
   Will see the world we know
   Gradually return'.

6. Listen to the silence of a snowy day. Think of the quietest thing in the world – is it a mouse on a misty morning? a caterpillar learning to crawl? a daisy closing its eye for the night? a bat's sneeze? Make a list of all the quietest things you can think of and put them into a picture called 'Silence'.

Movement and Drama:

1. Watch a group of children throwing and ducking away from snowballs (See Creative Activities, No. 3). Divide into two groups and make up an action dance of a snowball fight, using hand and arm for throwing, and bending the whole body to duck away from the snowballs. You might like to put music to this dance.
2. Look at the way animals move across the snow. Choose to be a particular animal or bird, and move shaking each paw like a cat stalking and placing each paw carefully like a fox, puffing up feathers like a robin. Let the others guess which animal or bird you are.
3. Read 'Any colour, as long as it's white'. Find out how many different things the child in the poem found to do in the snow. Mime all the things he did, and see if you can find other games that this child missed.

Frost and Ice

The Frozen Man

Out at the edge of town
where black trees

crack their fingers
in the icy wind

and hedges freeze
on their shadows

and the breath of cattle,
still as boulders,

hangs in rags
under the rolling moon,

a man is walking
alone:

on the coal-black road
his cold

feet
ring

and
ring.

Here in a snug house
at the heart of town

the fire is burning
red and yellow and gold:

you can hear the warmth
like a sleeping cat

breathe softly
in every room.

When the frozen man
comes to your door,

let him in,
let him in,
let him in.

Kit Wright

haiku

grass on the lawn
frost-thick. Facing my window
one fresh red rose.

Patricia Pogson

Christmas Album

Ice
turntable smooth
skaters cut grooves
with their blades
making music
as they slide, glide
spinning
around and around.

Michael Henry

Frost

I work while you sleep,
Needing no light to etch windows
Or elaborate leaf or branch.
Without colour my wonder is
My patterns within patterns
Growing like crisp stars.
Look, but do not touch.
Your warmth is my end.

John Cotton

Winter

Winter crept
through the whispering wood,
hushing fir and oak;
crushed each leaf and froze each web
but never a word he spoke.

Winter prowled
by the shivering sea,
lifting sand and stone;
nipped each limpet silently –
and then moved on.

Winter raced
down the frozen stream,
catching at his breath;
on his lips were icicles,
at his back was death.

Judith Nicholls

Old Winter

I have felt old Winter –
winter, in the air –
Have you heard him whispering?
Have you seen him there?

Ice upon his finger,
snow upon his back;
frosty are his footprints . . .
Can you mark his track?

I have known old Winter
many years, and more,
cool the fires of autumn –
a foot inside the door.

I have seen his silver
bright upon the bough,
and heard the owl: Whit-a-woo!
Winter's coming, now!

Jean Kenward

Frost and Ice

Discussion and Observation:

The first thing children want to do on any icy day is slide!

- Let them feel how slippery the ice is.
- Touch frost and ice with your fingers. Feel how cold it is, and how your fingers tingle when you get inside.
- Taste a touch of frost on your tongue. (Don't do this with ice – your tongue might stick. Why does this happen?)
- Look at frost patterns on windows. (See John Cotton's poem, 'Frost', – 'My patterns within patterns/Growing like crisp stars.')
- Look at the way twigs, fence tops and branches are outlined by frost.
- Look at grass whitened by frost.
- Watch what happens when the sun comes out.
- Listen to the silence of the first icy winter morning. (See Judith Nicholls' poem 'Winter', 'but never a word he spoke'.)
- Listen to children enjoying sliding and skating on the ice. (See Michael Henry's poem, 'Christmas Album'.)
- Watch what happens to ducks on an icy pond.
- Look at the way people dress against the cold and frost.
- Look at people's breath on a frosty morning.
- Listen to your footsteps on a frosty pavement.
- Melt a frost pattern on the window pane with your warm breath. ('Your warmth is my end.' John Cotton.)
- Look at the pattern of frost on fallen leaves. See how every vein is outlined. Lift some of the leaves and look at the dark earth beneath.

Classroom Activities:

1. Make ice cubes in the refrigerator. Feel them in your fingers and watch them melt. Take six cubes and place them in a container near a radiator. Put six others on the window sill. Put another six cubes outside in the playground. See how long it takes each lot to melt. What happens when the sun comes out?
2. Read Kit Wright's poem, 'The Frozen Man'. Talk about what you would do for him if you were able to ask him into the warmth of your own home. What are the best clothes to wear in the bitter cold? What is the best kind of food to eat to keep you warm and healthy? Make a list of all the things you would do to make the Frozen Man welcome.
3. Have you heard or read about people who have no homes to go to? There are some people who have to live rough and sleep in the streets, even in the depths of winter. Find newspaper photographs and cuttings about those who have to live rough. Think what it must be like to be on the outside looking into a warm brightly-lit house. Find out about the charities which help such people, e.g. Crisis at Christmas.

Language Activities:

1. Patricia Pogson has written her little poem to a special pattern called a haiku. A haiku is a three line poem in which you have to count the syllables. It should have five in the first line, seven in the second, and five in the third, making seventeen altogether. Do you think the poem has got it right? Try writing a haiku about winter. Look for a single image and describe it in three short lines.

Frost and Ice

2. Try writing an acrostic for winter weather. In an acrostic you read downwards so that the initial letters of each line form a name, a place, a season and so on. The poem should try to capture the characteristics of the person, place or kind of weather you are writing about.

   'Winter Playground'

   First frost;
   Run, slide, roll
   Over. Up again.
   Slide, sit down with a
   THUMP!

   Read the initial letters downwards and they make the word FROST. Try one with ICICLE, WINTER, CHRISTMAS.

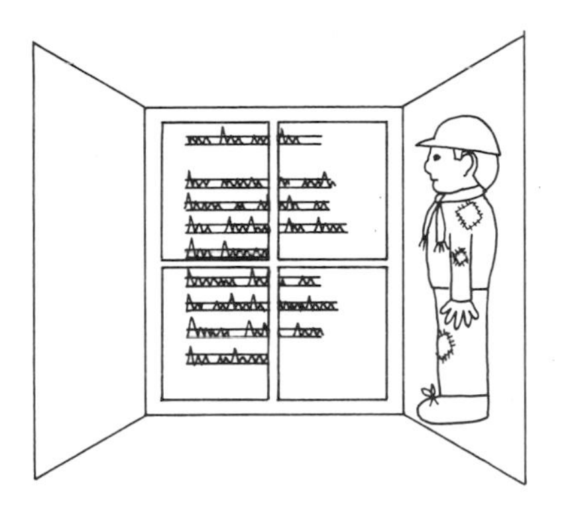

3. Read Kit Wright's poem, 'The Frozen Man'. (See Classroom Activities.) Imagine that you are on the outside, on a cold winter's night, looking into a warm bright room. You can see a family sitting by the heater, perhaps talking, reading or watching television. You can smell something delicious cooking for the evening meal. Don't forget, you are feeling hungry, cold and very much alone. Write a poem about how you feel being on the outside looking in. When your poem is finished, place it in the centre of your page. Staple an opening window over the poem, and draw yourself on the outside looking in, so that the poem fills the window space.
4. Read 'Winter' by Judith Nicholls. Imagine that you are an animal in the 'whispering wood' waiting for winter. You know that it can be a dangerous time for you ('on his lips were icicles/at his back was death'), so tell what preparations you must make, how you feel when you wake up to the first frosty morning, how you go about finding enough to eat.

Creative Activities:

1. Read 'Winter' by Judith Nicholls. (See Language Activities above.) Look outside at the shapes of bare winter trees. Draw those outlines on black, dark grey and light grey sugar paper and cut out. Now paste your tree shapes on to some dark blue paper, lighter trees at the back, black ones in the foreground. Make them overlap, so that you create a deep dark wood. Now use finger-painting to put frost on the tips of the branches and on the ground. Suggest some animals hiding in the woods by painting in a few shadowy shapes with bright shining eyes made from coloured foil scraps. Make the whole picture look mysterious and scary – a real 'whispering wood'.
2. Read Michael Henry's 'Christmas Album'. Work as a group, painting single skating figures in bright warm clothes. Look at the movements of the skaters, so that your figures look as though they 'slide, glide/ spinning/around and around'. Now make a background of a frozen pond. Make patterns on the ice where the skaters have 'cut grooves/with their blades'. Paste your figures on to the icy pond to make a bright winter picture, quite different from the gloomy 'whispering wood'.
3. Using felt-tip pens, make a window frame for the poem you have written from the ideas in Kit Wright's 'The Frozen Man'. (See Language Activities.) It must be a very cold scene, with the poem written on a lightly-crayonned background of reds and yellows to give the impression of warmth inside the room.
4. Find pictures of frost patterns. Use string dipped in white paint to make frost crystals or frosted spiders' webs. Use dark blue or purple paper as a background.

Fog

There's an old window cleaner
who only comes
when he's not wanted –
can't see to wash his cloth
and won't stop.
His name is Fog.
Geoffrey Holloway

Fog

The fog comes
on little cat feet.
It sits looking
over harbour and city
on silent haunches
and then moves on.
Carl Sandburg

Fog

Silent I invade cities,
Blur edges, confuse travellers,
My thumb smudging the light,
I drift from rivers
To loiter in early morning fields,
Until Constable Sun
Moves me on.
John Cotton

What is fog?

Puffs of dragon smoke
Curling round hedges and trees.

Clouds of steam from a giant's kettle
Pouring out over the city.

The breath from a dinosaur's nostrils
Blurring the world into a grey shadow.
John Foster

Fog

When I wake up in the morning
the dark fog is muttering.
It sulks around my window
like my best friend's worst bad mood.
But when I creep out to play with her,
to chase her frowns away,
the sun's got there before me
and fills the sky all day.
Dave Ward

The fog and me

It was so foggy today
that I couldn't see my hand
in front of my face.

I know
because I waved at myself
and I didn't wave back.
Ian McMillan

Fog

Discussion and Observation:

- Look from the classroom window at the unfamiliar shapes in the playground. Talk about how easy it would be to lose your way in the fog. Talk about the extra care needed by drivers, by children crossing the road on a foggy day. Now go outside warmly dressed.
- Look at the way fog hangs in the fields, the way animals loom out of the mist.
- Look at the halo effect of street lamps in the fog.
- Look at the way the sun can come up through the mist, the way the mist can lift, leaving a band of clear air above and below. (Read John Cotton's 'Fog'. Why does he talk about Constable Sun?)
- Listen to the muffled sounds of traffic, to children's voices echoing, to fog horns or ships' sirens, if the school is near the sea. (See Carl Sandburg's 'Fog'.)
- Touch the grass, leaves, stems of plants. Feel how soggy they are, how crisp if there is frost as well.
- Touch the car windscreen or the outside of the classroom window. See what dirt the fog can bring. (See Geoffrey Holloway's poem.)
- Listen to the silence of fog. ('Silent I invade cities . . .' from John Cotton's poem.)
- Talk about the different kinds of fog we experience, from a light mist like 'Puffs of dragon smoke' (John Foster's poem) to 'dark fog muttering' (from Dave Ward's poem). Talk about the smell of fog when you open the door.
- Look at the patterns on spiders' webs on a misty morning.

Classroom Activities:

1. Find a set of words to describe fog and mist. Print them white on grey, and cover with net or tissue paper to give a blurred effect. Use some of the words in the poems to start you off.
2. Talk about the need for extra care on roads on a foggy day. Talk about how to make ourselves, as pedestrians, more visible to drivers. Make suggestions for coats and armbands to wear on dark days. Find out which colours/materials show up best. Make a display of your own designs for easy-to-see clothes, with scraps of suitable materials (e.g. reflective plastic).
3. Find out about ships in fog. What kind of signals do they use? How do aircraft find their way in foggy conditions? What special advice is given to motorists who have to drive in fog?

   Pretend that you are an inventor. Design a device to help you find your way home in thick fog. It could be in the form of a map of landmarks which you can touch, or a simple length of string for you to follow – or it might be a special kind of fog light to wear on your head. Make it something that nobody has yet invented. Try to make your invention very exciting and unusual.
4. Organise a game of Blind Man's Bluff, or try to find your way blindfolded about the classroom. (Read Ian McMillan's poem, 'The fog and me'.)
5. Read Dave Ward's poem. He says that fog 'sulks round my window/like my best friend's worst bad mood.' See if you can think of moods that describe different kinds of weather. In a group, draw or paint a gallery of friends' faces with expressions (smiles/frowns/surprise) to match sunshine/storms/rain/clouds. Let the others in the class guess what kind of weather each face is supposed to be.

Fog

Language Activities:

1. Read all the poems you can find about fog to see how thinking about different animals helps us to describe what mist and fog is like. John Foster says that fog is like a dragon or a dinosaur. Carl Sandburg says that it is like a cat. Find other animals whose movements might suggest fog. Could fog be silent as a fox stealing through the night? Or like a bat flying across the dark? Find another description of your own, and put it into six lines like Carl Sandburg.
2. Have you ever been lost in a department store/in the attic/or on holiday? Imagine that you have been lost in the fog, and try to remember the abandoned feeling you had when losing sight of your parents. Describe how familiar things and places look different, how you gradually lose your bearings and how you feel when you realise you are lost. Make it into an adventure story. Will it have a happy ending?
3. Read John Foster's poem called 'What is fog?' In it he answers his own question in several different ways, simply putting together a list of ideas. Go out into the fog. Look and listen. Give everyone a slip of paper, and ask each person to answer John Foster's question in their own way. Then make up a group poem called 'What is fog?' by listing the ideas that each child has thought of. Print your poem on a dark blue or grey background and cut it into a shape that has no sharp edges. Make a border illustrating all the ideas in dark-coloured wax crayons.

Creative Activities:

1. Read John Foster's poem. Draw a picture of hedges and trees, grasses and bushes, by using white wax crayons or candles. Make it into a wax resist by giving it a wash with pale grey paint, to suggest mist 'curling round hedges and trees'.
2. Using the same poem as a starter, cut out the silhouettes of buildings, houses, tower blocks, church spires, in black paper. Overlay the buildings with torn white tissue paper pasted flat so that the edges of the buildings are blurred. Using white chalk on its side, make the fog rise like 'Clouds of steam from a giant's kettle. . .'
3. Read Carl Sandburg's poem. Using chalk and charcoal, draw a harbour scene. Remember to put in cranes, boats, masts – perhaps a bridge – and make the picture as mysterious and foggy as possible. It might be very effective to put a bright yellow/red sun in the corner, as though the fog is about to move on.
4. In a group, let each child paint a picture of him/herself in their brightest clothes. When the pictures are dry, cut them out and paste on to a grey background. Now experiment with scraps of net, tissue paper or cellophane to give a misty effect to the finished picture. Paste bright streaks of yellow sunlight beneath the net, as though, as in John Cotton's poem, fog 'smudges the light'.

Drama and Mime:

1. Find as many animals as you can whose movements suggest fog and mist. Now move about the hall as these animals might move. Make it all very slow and mysterious, like a slowed-down television replay. Look for words in the poems which describe the movements of fog, e.g. 'drift', 'loiter', 'sulk'.
2. Imagine you are lost in the fog. In groups, develop short mimes of losing your way home, asking directions of people you meet, at last realising that you are in your own street, opening your own front door.

For details of further Belair publications
please write to:

BELAIR PUBLICATIONS LTD.
P.O. Box 12,
TWICKENHAM
TW1 2QL.
England.